AF600153

THE CATHOLIC UNIVERSITY OF AMERICA
CANON LAW STUDIES
No. 394

The Rites and Ceremonies of Sacred Ordination

(Canons 1002-1005)

A Historical Conspectus and a Canonical Commentary

A DISSERTATION

Submitted to the Faculty of the School of Canon Law of The Catholic University of America in Partial Fulfillment of the Requirements for the Degree of Doctor of Canon Law

BY

WALTER B. CLANCY, J.C.L.
A priest of the Diocese of Little Rock

THE CATHOLIC UNIVERSITY OF AMERICA PRESS
WASHINGTON, D. C.
1962

The Rites and Ceremonies of Sacred Ordination

This dissertation was approved by the Very Rev. Clement V. Bastnagel, S.T.L., J.U.D., Dean of the School of Canon Law, as director, and the Rev. Romaeus W. O'Brien, O.Carm., J.C.D., and the Rev. Fredrick R. McManus, A.B., J.C.D., as readers.

THE CATHOLIC UNIVERSITY OF AMERICA
CANON LAW STUDIES
No. 394

The Rites and Ceremonies of Sacred Ordination

(Canons 1002-1005)

A Historical Conspectus and a Canonical Commentary

A DISSERTATION

Submitted to the Faculty of the School of Canon Law of The Catholic University of America in Partial Fulfillment of the Requirements for the Degree of Doctor of Canon Law

BY

WALTER B. CLANCY, J.C.L.
A priest of the Diocese of Little Rock

THE CATHOLIC UNIVERSITY OF AMERICA PRESS
WASHINGTON, D. C.
1962

Nihil Obstat:

CLEMENS V. BASTNAGEL, S.T.L., J.U.D.
Censor Deputatus

Washingtonii, die 5 iunii, 1961

Imprimatur:

ALBERTUS L. FLETCHER, D.D.
Episcopus Petriculanus

Petriculae die 15 iunii, 1961

Printed by
THE WICKERSHAM PRINTING CO.
Lancaster, Pennsylvania

To My Mother and Father

FOREWORD

Our Lord, in founding His Church as a hierarchical society, also provided for the perpetuation of His Mystical Body in time. Through the sacrament of Orders the powers He entrusted to His first disciples have passed to each succeeding generation to form again a source of grace for the ministering of divine worship and the government of the faithful. The acts by which these essential powers are conferred have developed, in the course of the centuries, into the elaborate and familiar rituals used by the Church today. It is these acts and the laws enacted to insure the valid and lawful transfer of these powers which the writer plans to investigate in treating of the rites and ceremonies of sacred ordination.

The title of this study will be recognized as that of the fourth chapter of the section treating of the sacrament of Holy Orders in the Code of Canon Law. The four canons gathered under that chapter heading will furnish the subject matter to be treated in the pages that follow. For purposes of clarity and convenience the treatment of these canons will be divided into two parts. The first will be concerned solely with the rites and ceremonies as such, that is, as they are applied by the minister in the very act of ordination. No attempt, however, will be made to outline the ceremonial actions of the minister in detail; such a study belongs to a field other than canon law. Here the general obligation of the minister of sacred ordination will be considered in the light of canon 1002. Once this obligation has been established, there will follow an investigation of what may be called the negative and more particular aspect of the minister's obligation, namely, the repair of defective rites. The basic problem here of establishing the norms of valid and lawful ordination will necessitate a rather lengthy excursus into the history of the sacrament of Orders. These norms will then be applied to each of the major Orders for the purpose of determining the specific obligation of the minister in those unfortunate cases wherein the rites of ordination are defectively applied. The second part of this study will treat of the Mass of Ordination and of the supplying of minor Orders in those cases wherein a member of an Oriental Rite receives further Orders in the Latin discipline.

The writer wishes to express his sincere gratitude to His Excellency, the Most Reverend Albert L. Fletcher, D.D., Bishop of Little Rock, for the opportunity to pursue graduate studies in Canon Law at the Catholic University of America. He also wishes to thank the members of the Faculty of the School of Canon Law, his classmates and his friends, for their kind assistance and encouragement in the preparation of this work.

TABLE OF CONTENTS

PAGE

CHAPTER 6

PART I

THE OBLIGATION OF THE MINISTER IN CONFERRING SACRED ORDINATION (CANON 1002)

INTRODUCTION

Since the night of the Last Supper, when Our Lord gave to His Apostles and to His Church the Christian Priesthood with the words, "Do this in commemoration of Me," [1] the august sacrament of Orders has commanded the attention of the Church as one of the most precious of the gifts entrusted to its care. In enacting laws for the protection and preservation of this most vital institution, the Church has not neglected to give consideration to the rites and ceremonies by which it is conferred. These many laws are incorporated in and made a part of the canonical legislation of the Church in canon 1002, where the minister of Orders is enjoyed with the strict obligation of accurately observing, unchanged and in their entirety, the proper rites of ordination as described in the Roman Pontifical and other liturgical books.[2]

In addition to this general obligation, another particular or reparative obligation can arise when any one of the individual rites has been omitted or has been performed defectively. Both areas of responsibility will be treated in the pages that follow.

The testimony of history will contribute liberally to giving the reader a clearer notion of the problems involved and to helping him approach their solution. A survey of the history of the development of the rites and ceremonies of sacred ordination will be presented by way of introduction.

The Code of Canon Law uses the term *sacra ordinatio* to include, besides major and minor Orders, also episcopal consecration and first clerical tonsure.[3] This first part will be restricted

[1] Luke, XXII: 19; Sessio XXII, *Doctrina de Sacrificio Missae,* Canon 2—Schroeder, *Canons and Decrees of the Council of Trent* (St. Louis: Herder and Co., 1941), pp. 149, 412.

[2] "In quovis conferendo ordine, minister proprios ritus in Pontificali Romano aliisve ritualibus libris ab Ecclesia probatis descriptos, adamussim servet, quos nulla ratione licet praeterire vel invertere."

[3] Canon 951.

to an investigation of only the major or sacred Orders and episcopal consecration. The advisability of this course of action is evident. The minor Orders, as institutions of ecclesiastical law, can be changed and their powers supplied by the Church at will. The major Orders will be considered only as they are conferred in the Latin Rite.

CHAPTER 1

A HISTORY OF THE DEVELOPMENT OF THE RITES OF SACRED ORDINATION

The history of the development of the rites of sacred ordination is but one aspect of the history of the evolution of the Roman Liturgy. During its formative period every age and nation made particular contributions to the embellishment of the essential and unchangeable elements of the Catholic liturgy. Andrieu (1886-1957) remarked that this was one of the contributing factors for the unity of the liturgical discipline in the west.[4] Each nation recognized in the rites of the Roman Church something of its own national character. These influences are evident in the present ordination ceremony. In this brief outline there will be given only those details which are necessary for an explanation regarding the origin of the rites, or for a fixing of the time in history when a particular practice was first accepted by the Church. The former will be useful for a consideration of the varied opinions of canonists and theologians with reference to the essential rites of each of the Orders; the latter will find importance in the establishing of an early norm of law in this field where, in the face of a near-absence of positive legislation, the customary law predominated.[5]

Article I. The Apostolic Age

Although Christ called His disciples to the priesthood without any specific ceremony,[6] soon after His ascension there appeared the first rudiment of an external rite for the conferring of the

[4] *Le Pontifical Romain de Moyen Age* (4 vols., Città del Vaticano: Biblioteca Apostolica Vaticana, 1938-1941), Vol. I, *Le Pontifical de XII Siècle,* p. 8.

[5] Cf. Oppenheim, *Institutiones Systematico-Historicae in Sacram Liturgicam* (Series I, 6 vols., Taurini: Marietti, 1937-1941), Vol. I, *Tractatus de Iure Liturgico,* Pars I, pp. 20-21.

[6] Luke, XXII:19; I Cor., XI:24.

power of Orders: the imposition of hands.[7] In the sixth chapter of the Acts, the disciples, at the bidding of the Apostles, chose seven deacons. "These were set before the Apostles; and they praying, imposed hands upon them." [8] The two elements discernible in this unique description of the Apostolic rite, that is, the outward gesture of imposing hands and the recitation of a prayer, form the substance of the rite of ordination as subsequently developed.[9]

Article II. St. Hippolytus of Rome

A description of the rites of ordination appears in one of the richest sources of the primitive liturgy of Rome, *The Apostolic Tradition of St. Hippolytus of Rome.*[10] The full ceremony is given for ordination to the episcopate, to the priesthood, and to the diaconate.[11] Each contains three elements: An election, the

[7] II Tim., I:6; Acts, VI:6; I Tim., V:22; I Tim., IV:4.

[8] Acts, VI:6.

[9] "The rite of inauguration of the sacred ministers of the Church was always and everywhere the laying on of hands. Indeterminate in itself, the rite receives its precise signification from the circumstances which surround it or from the words which accompany it. We see in Scripture that hands are laid on, by the superior to bless, by the worker of miracles to heal, by the Apostles to confer the Holy Ghost, and by those endowed with ecclesiastical authority to communicate the power with which they are invested."—Prat, *The Theology of Saint Paul,* translated from the tenth French edition by John L. Stoddard (2 vols., Westminster, Maryland: The Newman Press, 1952), II, 268.

[10] The text of this document was found early in the past century and was originally referred to as *The Egyptian Church Order.* Research has identified the author and the circumstances which surrounded his writing. The latter indicate that this work reflects the Roman Liturgy of the second half of the second century or earlier. Cf. Quasten, *Patrology* (3 vols., Westminster, Maryland: The Newman Press, 1951-1960), II, 180-194; the classical text is that of Hauler, *Didascaliae Apostolorum Fragmenta Veronensia* . . (Lipsiae, 1900), pp. 103-110. This text is reprinted by Lennerz in his *De Sacramento Ordinis* (Editio secunda, Romae: Apud Aedes Universitatis Gregorianae, 1953), pp. 13-14; an English translation is edited by Dom Gregory Dix, *The Treatise of the Apostolic Tradition of St. Hippolytus of Rome* (London: The Society for Promoting Christian Knowledge—New York: Macmillan, 1937).

[11] Cf. Otterbein, *The Diaconate According to the Apostolic Tradition of Hippolytus and Derived Documents* (The Catholic University of America

laying on of hands and the accompanying prayer. The various Orders are distinguished by the prayer and by the manner in which the hands are imposed. In the consecration of a bishop it is only the bishops who impose hands; the priests stand by in silence.[12] In the ordination of priests all the priests present follow after the bishop in imposing hands upon the one who receives ordination, but it is clear that only the bishop ordains.[13] When a deacon is ordained, only the bishop imposes hands, for, as St. Hippolytus († 235) explained, he is not to be ordained a priest.[14]

A consecratory prayer is given for each of the Orders. In speaking of the ordination of confessors for the faith, however, St. Hippolytus furnished an interesting commentary on the attitude of the early Church towards the formulation of the prayer used in the rite of ordination.

> It is not altogether necessary for him to recite the very same words which we gave before as though studying to say them by heart in his thanksgiving to God; but let each one pray according to his own ability. If indeed he on the other hand shall pray and receive a prayer according to a fixed form, no one shall prevent him, only let his prayer be correct and right (in doctrine).[15]

This lack of insistence on a rigidly fixed formula at that time in the history of the Church can be well understood in the light of other liturgical developments. A fixed dogmatic framework within which the minister used his own words was rather to be expected.[16]

The Apostolic Tradition had no appreciable effect on the de-

Studies in Sacred Theology, p. 95, Washington, D. C.: The Catholic University of America Press, 1945), pp. 41-56; the first recorded mention of the subdiaconate is believed to be found in later Coptic and Arabic versions of the *Traditio Apostolica.*—Lennerz, *op. cit.,* p. 15.

12 Dix, *op. cit.,* p. 2.

13 *Ibid.,* p. 17.

14 *Ibid.,* p. 15.

15 *Ibid.,* p. 19.

16 Jungmann, *The Mass of the Roman Rite: Its Origins and Development,* translated from the second (revised) edition of the German by Francis A. Brunner (2 vols., New York: Benziger Brothers, 1950-1955), I, 30.

velopment of the rite of ordination in the west.[17] It is important, however, as furnishing practically the only account of the practices of the Roman Church before the fourth century.

Article III. The Early Roman Tradition

The Church emerged from the persecutions of the third and early fourth centuries with a territorial organization modeled largely after the political provinces of the Empire. Diocletian (284-305) was responsible for the political division between the East and the West which even in the fourth century had its counterpart in the diverse liturgical usages current in Rome on the one hand and in Constantinople on the other.

In the West the pre-eminence of the Roman Church in matters of liturgical discipline was given firm expression by Pope Innocent I (401-417) in a letter addressed to the Bishop of Gubbio in the district of Umbria in the year 416. The Roman Pontiff warned against liturgical innovation, especially in the rites of ordination, and insisted on conformity to the Apostolic Tradition as found in the Church of Rome. He began his letter with this admonition:

> If the Priests of the Lord wish to preserve in their entirety the ecclesiastical institutions, as they were handed down by the blessed apostles, *let there be no diversity, no variety in Orders and Consecrations*. . . .Who cannot know, who would not notice that what was handed down to the Roman Church by Peter, the Prince of the Apostles, is preserved even until now and ought to be observed by all, and that nothing ought to be changed or introduced without this authority . . . (emphasis added).[18]

[17] Quasten, *op. cit.*, II, 181.

[18] "Si instituta ecclesiastica, ut sunt a beatis apostolis tradita, integra valent servare domini sacerdotes, nulla diversitas, nulla varietas in ipsis ordinibus et consecrationibus haberetur. . Quis enim nesciat aut non advertat, id quod a principe Apostolorum Petro Romanae Ecclesias traditum est, ac nunc usque custoditur, ab omnibus debere servari; nec super [in]duci aut introduci aliquid, quod auctoritatem non habeat. . . " Migne, *Patrologiae Cursus Completus, Series Latina* (221 vols., Parisiis, 1844-1864), XX, 551-552 (hereafter cited as *MPL*); Mansi, *Sacrorum Conciliorum Nova et Amplissima Collectio* (53 vols. in 60, Parisiis, 1901-1927), III, 1028 (hereafter cited as Mansi); Jaffé, *Regesta Pontificum Romanorum ab condita Ecclesia ad annum post Christum natum MCXCVIII* (ed. 2, correctam

The earliest reflection of this tradition in the development of the rites of sacred ordination is found in the oldest of the Roman Sacramentaries and Ordinals. The former were collections of prayers used by the bishops and priests in the celebration of the liturgy; the latter were the books of rubrics and instructions used in conjunction with the Sacramentaries. The two together form the original source of the missal and pontifical in use today.[19]

Two of the Sacramentaries stand out as the most ancient. The *Leonine Sacramentary,*[20] preserved in a single manuscript from the sixth century[21] and representing the tradition, if not the actual work, of St. Leo the Great (446-461),[22] and the *Gregorian Sacramentary*, which may be assigned approximately to the same date.[23] The latter Sacramentary, in its original form, was probably compiled by Pope Gregory the Great (590-604) from an even older Sacramentary ascribed to Pope Gelasius (492-496).[24] The Ordinals, also Roman in origin, present a tradition that in its oldest form can be dated as early as the seventh century.[25]

---

et auctam auspiciis Gulielmi Wattenbach curaverunt F. Kaltanbrunner [ad annum 590], P. Ewald [590-882], S. Loewenfeld [882-1198], 2 vols., Lipsiae, 1885-1888), n. 311 (hereafter cited JK, JE, JL).

19 De Puniet, *The Roman Pontifical, A History and Commentary,* translated by Mildred V. Harcourt (London–New York–Toronto: Longmans, Green and Co., 1932), p. 12.

20 The more important editions are: Mohlberg, *Sacramentarium Veronense,* Rerum Ecclesiasticarum Documenta, cura Pontificii Athenaei S. Anselmi in Urbe edita, Series maior, Fontes, I (Roma: Casa Editrice Herder, 1956); Feltoe, *Sacramentarium Leonianum* (Cambridge: University Press, 1896); Muratori, *Liturgia Romana Vetus* (2 vols., Venetiis, 1784), I, 288-484, reproducing the edition of the Ballerini brothers; also in *MPL,* LV, 21-156.

21 Jungmann, *op. cit.,* I, 61.

22 Kennedy, *The Saints of the Canon of the Mass,* Studi di Antichità Cristiana, XIV (Città del Vaticano: Pontificio Instituto de Archeologia Cristiana, 1938), pp. 32-33.

23 Jungmann, *op. cit.,* I, 63. An edition of the full Sacramentary can be found in *MPL,* LXXVII, 25-240; cf. also Muratori, *op. cit.,* II, 406-414.

24 John the Deacon, *Vita S. Gregorii,* II, 17.—*MPL,* LXXV, 94.

25 Jungmann, *op. cit.,* I, 66. The classical edition of the *Ordines Romani* is that of Mabillon, who includes fifteen ordinals of different periods in his

The rites presented in these collections for the major Orders and the episcopate follow the same general pattern. An outline of the consecration of a bishop will serve to exemplify the simplicity that was still a characteristic of the Roman ceremony.

After the candidate had been presented to the pope and approved by him, two very brief prayers were read over the bishop-elect. These prayers were separated by the people's chanting of the litany and followed by the consecratory prayer, "*Vere dignum est . . . comple in sacerdotibus tuis mysterii tui summam, et ornamentis totius glorificationis instructos caelestis unguenti fluore sanctifica.*" This formula, which is contained in both the Leonine Sacramentary [26] and the Gregorian,[27] is almost identical with the words found in the preface used in the present rite of consecration. During the prayer the pope imposed hands upon the candidate, who then, after receiving the kiss of peace from the pope, took his place within the ranks of the bishops.[28]

In the ordination of priests and deacons the imposition of hands and the consecratory prayer were always part of the rite. The candidates were usually clothed in the vestments proper to each of the Orders before the ceremony began; Ordinal IX, however, points to the delivery of the vestments of the priest during the ordination. The stole was given by the archdeacon; the chasuble by the bishop.[29]

The Order of the subdiaconate was not considered a major

Museum Italicum. This is reproduced in *MPL,* LXXVIII, 1001-1008. A new critical edition has been edited by Andrieu, *Les Ordines Romani du Haut Moyen Age* (3 vols., Louvain: Spicilegium Sacrum Lovaniense, 1931-1951).

26 Mohlberg, *Sacramentarium Veronense,* p. 119.

27 *MPL,* LV, 114.

28 Ordo IX, n. 4: "Canunt litaniam; et tunc accedit (electus) propius ad altare subnixo capite. Pontifex vero ponit manum super caput ejus, et dicit unam orationem in modum collectae, alteram eo modulamine quo solet contestata cantari, et sedet pontifex in sella sua. Ipse vero osculatur pedem ejus, et suscipitur ad pacem, et sic consummatur consecratio illius." —*MPL,* LXXVIII, 1006; Andrieu (*Les Ordines Romani du Haut Moyen Age,* I, 19) refers to this work as Ordo XXXVI.

29 *MPL,* LXXXVIII, 1005.

Order until the time of Pope Innocent III (1198-1216),[30] and as a minor Order was almost completely ignored in the early Roman Sacramentaries. There was no solemn rite. The subdeacon approached the bishop during the Mass and was handed an empty chalice. A simple blessing was pronounced over him by the bishop.[31]

ARTICLE IV. THE GALLICAN CONTRIBUTION

The confusion and disintegration that followed upon the fall of the Roman Empire of the West (c. 475) and the migration of the Germanic nations brought to a halt any interchange of influence between Rome and the transalpine liturgy proper to Gaul. When Charlemagne ascended the throne of the Frankish Empire, the deplorable state of the Gallican Liturgy prompted him to request of the reigning Pontiff copies of the Sacramentaries in use in Rome. Pope Hadrian (772-795) replied to his request between the years 784 and 791 by sending copies of the Sacramentary compiled by Pope Gregory the Great (590-604).[32] This and other basically Roman texts were combined with the traditions of the Gallican Church to form a composite rite, which was to have much influence on the development of the rites of ordination.[33] The more important of the Gallican texts available are:

1. The *Statuta Ecclesiae Antiqua,* which probably originated in the province of Arles around the middle of the fifth century.[34]

[30] C. 9, X, *de aetate et qualitate et ordine praeficiendorum,* 1, 14.

[31] Duchesne, *Christian Worship: Its Origin and Evolution,* translated from the 5. French ed. by M. L. McClure (London: Society for Promoting Christian Knowledge, 1920), pp. 352-353 (hereafter cited *Christian Worship*).

[32] *MPL,* XCVIII, 434; Mansi, XII, 798; JE, n. 2473.

[33] Wilson, *The Gregorian Sacramentary (Under Charles the Great),* edited from 3 Mss. of the ninth century (London, 1915), p. xxii; De Puniet, *op. cit.,* pp. 21-22.

[34] Van Hove, *Prolegomena ad Codicem Iuris Canonici* (2. ed. Mechliniae–Romae: Dessain, 1945), p. 125. The complete text is found under the inscription of the IV Council of Carthage in Mansi, III, 949. This collection was for a long time accepted as genuine conciliar legislation, having passed from the Spanish body of the canons (*Hispana*) to the pseudo-Isidorian Decretals through the carelessness of a copyist who came in contact with the *Statuta* shortly after the acts of the IV Council of Carthage.

2. The *Gelasian Sacramentary of the Eighth Century,* which shows an admixture of Roman and Gallican rites in use in the seventh century.[35]

3. The *Missale Francorum,* exhibiting the same admixture of rites, which derives from a manuscript belonging to the end of the seventh or the beginning of the eighth century.[36]

4. The *Pontifical of Egbert* (c. 750), which reflects the usage of the English Church.[37]

The full extent of the contribution made by the Gallican Church to the rite of ordination can best be seen through a consideration of the additions made to each of the Orders in turn.

In the consecration of a bishop the *Statuta Ecclesiae Antiqua* prescribed that two bishops were to place the book of the gospels on the head and shoulders of the bishop-elect while the bishop consecrator said the prayers over the candidate. All the other bishops present were to impose hands upon the head of the one being consecrated.[38] Although no mention is made regarding the imposition of hands by the principal bishop consecrator, this action was always inseparably joined with the prayer of consecration.[39] Amalarius († 851), Chorbishop in the diocese of Metz and a prominent writer in the field of liturgical reform, objected that the *traditio* of the book of the gospels was neither of ancient

[35] Many, *Praelectiones de Sacra Ordinatione* (Parisiis: Letouzey et Ané, 1905), p. 441. The full text is found in *MPL,* LXXIV, 1049-1244.

[36] Tixeront, *Holy Orders and Ordination,* translated from the second French edition by S. A. Raemers (St. Louis–London: E. Herder, 1928), p. 168.

[37] Martène, *De Antiquis Ecclesiae Ritibus* (3 vols., Venetiis, 1783), I, 31-36.

[38] "Episcopus cum ordinatur, duo episcopi ponant et teneant evangeliorum codicem super caput et cervicem eius, et uno super eum fundente benedictionem reliqui omnes episcopi, qui adsunt, manibus suis caput tangant."—Mansi, III, 951; Denzinger-Bannwart-Umberg-Rahner, *Enchiridion Symbolorum Definitionum et Declarationum de Rebus Fidei et Morum* (30. ed., Friburgi–Brisgoviae: B. Herder and Co., 1955), n. 150 (hereafter cited *Enchiridion*).

[39] Schuster, *The Sacramentary, Historical and Liturgical Notes on the Roman Missal,* Translated from the Italian by Arthur Levelis-Marke (5 vols., New York: Benziger Bros., 1924-1930), I, 129.

authority, nor of Apostolic tradition, nor of canonical authority.[40]

This same writer, however, was responsible for encouraging the introduction of another ceremony in the rite of consecration, which was equally without the authority of tradition: the use of oil for anointing. In his great work, *De Officiis Ecclesiae* (827), Amalarius pointed to the anointing of the sons of Aaron [41] as authority for the anointing used in the ordination rites of his day.[42] Ellard, who has made an extensive study of the use of oil in the ordination rites of the Western Church, maintains that Amalarius "under the guise of relating what was current usage, is deliberately pleading for the general introduction of anointing at Holy Orders." [43] This practice of anointing the head and the hands of the bishop was reflected in the *Pontifical of Egbert,* [44] and gradually spread from the English Church to the Continent. The custom of anointing was not found in Rome, however, until the Pontificate of Pope John X (914-928).[45] The delivery of the pontifical insignia was the customary practice of the Spanish Church, according to the testimony of St. Isidore († 636),[46] but the capping with the miter did not appear until the twelfth century.

The antiquity of the imposition of hands with the consecratory prayer as a part of the rite of priestly ordination has been established, as has been the delivery of the stole and the chasuble. The Gallican Church added to these the anointing of hands and the delivery of the chalice and paten. The use of oil for anointing is first found in the *Missale Francorum* [47] and was in common use in Gaul by the ninth century.[48]

[40] *De Officiis Ecclesiae,* Cap. XIV.—*MPL,* CV, 1096.

[41] Exodus, XXIX:7.

[42] *Loc. cit.*

[43] Ellard, *Ordination Anointings in the Western Church before 1000 A.D.* (Mediaeval Studies, n. 31: Cambridge, Mass., 1933), p. 40.

[44] Martène, *op. cit.,* I, 32.

[45] Ellard, *op. cit.,* p. 40.

[46] *De Ecclesiasticis Officiis,* Lib. II, Cap. 9.—*MPL,* LXXXIII, 783-784.

[47] Muratori, *Liturgia Romana Vetus,* II, 669.

[48] Many, *op. cit.,* p. 419.

The introduction of the use of the chalice and paten was to have much more importance in the formation of the full rite of ordination for, as will be seen, many in following St. Thomas thought this to be the essential rite through which the power of Orders was received. The exact date when this ceremony began to be used is uncertain. Neither Isidore nor Amalarius made mention of its use. The first vestige of the use of the chalice and paten in an ordination rite is found in a Gregorian Sacramentary preserved in the Vatican library, in a rubric for the consecration of a bishop.[49] This ceremony with the accompanying formula, "*Accipe potestatem offerre sacrificium Deo . . . ,*" was probably added to the rite of ordination for a priest around the tenth century to give more solemnity to the ceremony and to furnish a more tangible expression of the powers received at ordination.[50] While no ecclesiastical writers make mention of this ceremony during the following century,[51] Hugh of St. Victor († 1141) testified to its common use in Gaul in the twelfth century.[52]

The last addition to the rite of priestly ordination, the final imposition of hands, is not properly a contribution of the Gallican Church, for it appeared after the fusion of the Gallican and Roman Liturgies. Nevertheless, for the sake of completeness, it will be discussed here. William Durantis (1237-1296) included this ceremony in his pontifical and is probably responsible for its use in the rite of ordination today. The origin of this practice, however, must be found elsewhere. A marginal note in the Rheims Pontifical of the twelfth century gives some indication of the beginning of this practice.[53] The words, "*Accipe Spiritum Sanctum, quorum remiseritis peccata . . . ,*" are written in after the tradition of the chalice and wine and before the complete unfolding of the chasuble. Arguing from the later development in

[49] Van Rossum, *De Essentia Sacramenti Ordinis* (2. ed., Romae: Fridericus Pustet, 1931), p. 133, n. 283.

[50] Bligh, *Ordination to the Priesthood* (New York: Sheed and Ward, 1955), p. 137.

[51] Van Rossum, *op. cit.*, p. 153, nn. 339-343.

[52] *De Sacramentis*, Lib. II, p. 3, c. 12.—*MPL*, CLXXVI, 429.

[53] Van Rossum, *op. cit.*, p. 145, n. 315.

the rite, these words probably accompanied a second imposition of hands. This action could have been added to make the whole rite adhere more closely to the scriptural account of the conferral of power on the Apostles by Our Lord. Bligh conjectures that the prayer accompanying the imposition of hands, the *"Accipe Spiritum Sanctum . . . ,"* originally was said with the first imposition and was completed in a fashion more expressive of the form of the Order than the *"quorum remiseris peccata, remittuntur eis . . ."* which came to be used. This formula was then transferred with a second imposition of hands to a position in the ceremony after the communion to complete the form or shape of the ceremony. This took place at some unspecified date between the eleventh and thirteenth centuries.[54]

In the ordination of deacons the delivery of the stole and alb appear as a subject of legislation in the IV Council of Toledo (633),[55] but the custom did not take root in the Gallican Church until the ninth century. The dalmatic, because of its special significance in papal ceremonies, did not come into use until much later.[56] The first mention of the handing of the book of the gospels was made in the *Pontifical of Egbert,* which also records the prayer, *"Accipe istud volumen evangelii, et lege, et intellege, et aliis trade, et tu opere adimple."*[57] The acceptance of this rite came very slowly also, for Peter Lombard (1100-1160) remembered this ceremony as having been introduced during his lifetime.[58] The custom of anointing the hands of the deacon with oil, which for a time flourished in the Gallican Church, was reprobated by Pope Nicholas I (858-867) as opposed to the use of the Church of Rome, and thus it ceased, after a time, to be a part of the rite of ordination for deacons.[59]

Duchesne (1843-1922) gave this description of the ordination to the subdiaconate:

[54] Bligh, *op. cit.,* pp. 163-165.

[55] Canon 28.—Mansi, X, 627.

[56] *Dictum* post c. 9, D. XXIII.

[57] Martène, *op. cit.,* I, 32.

[58] *Sent., Lib. IV,* Dic. 24, n. 8.—*MPL,* CXCII, 90.

[59] C. 12, D. XXIII. The original letter is found in *MPL,* CXIX, 884.

> The Ordination of the subdeacon among the Franks was quite simple also. The bishop gave him the chalice and the paten; then the archdeacon presented the basin and napkin for drying the hands. Before the *traditio* of these objects the bishop delivered a short address, and afterwards read two short prayers of blessing.[60]

This is basically the ceremony given in the *Statuta Ecclesiae Antiqua*.[61] No significant development took place in this ceremony until it came to be numbered among the major Orders around the year 1198. The ceremonies of the delivery of the book and of the bestowal of the amice were probably added by William Durantis.[62]

Article V. The Roman Pontifical

The Pontifical, as a book of prayers and ceremonies normally reserved for the use of the bishop, was not known at Rome until the tenth century. With the restoration of the Empire under Otto I (962) the center of liturgical development moved from France to the banks of the Rhine. There the tendency to collect and give order to the books of the liturgy bore fruit. The Monks of the Benedictine Abbey of St. Alban in Mainz were among the first to produce a liturgical book exclusively for episcopal ceremonies (ca. 950). This German Collection, together with many others, crossed the Alps with the bishops in the trains of the Saxon Princes and quickly replaced the ancient local rites of the Church of Rome.[63] It was through this *Mainz Pontifical,* or as it came to be called, the *Romano-Germanic Pontifical,* that the many additions to the rites of ordination as developed in the Gallican Church were accepted and became the practice of the Church in Rome.[64]

The next major contribution to the formation of the pontifical was made by William Durantis (1237-1296), a celebrated canonist and liturgist of the Roman Curia. After his election to the

[60] *Christian Worship,* pp. 367-368.

[61] Canon 5.—Mansi, III, 949.

[62] De Puniet, *The Roman Pontifical,* pp. 165-167.

[63] Andrieu, *Le Pontifical Roman du Moyen Age,* I, 3-5.

[64] *Loc. cit.*

see of Mende, he undertook on his own authority a revision of the *Pontifical of the Roman Curia* then in use in Rome, with a view to bringing more order into the espicopal ceremonies.[65] Under the influence of Scholasticism with its emphasis on logical division, he divided the whole pontifical into three parts. The first book dealt with persons, the second with liturgical objects, and the third with lesser rites and ceremonies. The rites of ordination were given a place of importance immediately after confirmation in the first book.[66] His contribution to the rites themselves was more one of arrangement than one of addition, although, as has been seen, he did not leave the rites totally undisturbed. The *Romano-Germanic Pontifical* shows the ceremonies of ordination gathered in one place at the end of the Tract. Durantis divided the rites for the conferral of the priesthood into two parts, placing the final imposition of hands and a promise of obedience after the communion. This pontifical became widely accepted in the course of the fourteenth and fifteenth centuries,[67] and gave the final form to our present rite of ordination.

The first official edition of the Roman Pontifical was compiled by Bishop Augustine Patrizi († 1496) under instructions from Pope Innocent VIII (1484-1492).[68] The work of Patrizi was but a slightly altered version of the *Pontifical of Durantis*, excluding certain rites that had fallen into desuetude, but adding others that were in current use. The rubrics governing the bishop's actions while officiating were standardized. This *Pontificalis Liber*, as it was called, was approved by Innocent VIII and printed in Rome in 1485.[69]

The advent of printing put an end to private initiative in this field; new editions of the Roman Pontifical appeared only with

65 Andrieu, *Le Pontifical Romain du Moyen Age*, Vol. III, *Le Pontifical de Guillaume Durand*, pp. 9-12.

66 *Ibid.*, III, 358-364.

67 De Puniet, *op. cit.*, p. 28.

68 *Ibid.*, pp. 44-45.

69 Cabrol, *The Books of the Latin Liturgy*, translated from the French by the Benedictines of Stanbrook (St. Louis: B. Herder and Co., 1932), p. 57.

the authority of the Roman Pontiff. Under the influence of the Council of Trent (1545-1563) [70] the first official and exclusive version of the *Pontificale Romanum* was promulgated. Clement VIII (1592-1605), in the Constitution *Ex quo in Ecclesia Dei,* dated February 10, 1596, suppressed all private pontificals and made the Roman Pontifical obligatory throughout the Western Church.[71]

Further official revisions of the pontifical appeared during the reigns of Urban VIII (1623-1644), Benedict XIII (1724-1730), Benedict XIV (1740-1758) and Leo XIII (1878-1903), with little change being made in the rites of ordination.[72] Only recently Pius XII has seen fit to make certain modifications in the rubrics of the Roman Pontifical. On November 30, 1944, he issued an Apostolic Constitution to clarify the role and duties of the assisting bishops in the rite of episcopal consecration.[73] The rubrics were ordered to be duly revised to conform to these prescriptions. The Apostolic Constitution *Sacramentum Ordinis* concerning the essential rites of the three higher orders also occasioned detailed changes in the rubrics drawn up for these ordinations.[74] A decree of the Congregation of Sacred Rites, dated February 20, 1950, listed these additions and variations, and also indicated the manner in which the sacramental forms are to be printed in the future.[75]

* * *

Thus has the simple apostolic rite of the imposition of hands grown to the elaborate and symbolic ceremony used in the Church today. The words of John Morinus (1591-1659), the great his-

[70] Sessio XXV, *Continuatio Sessionis, De Indice Librorum et Catechismo, Breviario et Missali.*—Schroeder, *Canons and Decrees of the Council of Trent,* pp. 254-255; 519-520.

[71] De Puniet, *op. cit.,* p. 31.

[72] *Ibid.,* pp. 51-52; Oppenheim, *op. cit.,* IV, P. III (1940), 115-116.

[73] *Acta Apostolicae Sedis, Commentarium Officiale* (Romae, 1909-1929; Civitate Vaticana, 1929-), XXXVII (1945), 131 (hereafter cited *AAS*). Cf. *infra,* p. 96.

[74] *AAS,* XL (1948), 5-7. Cf. *infra,* p. 100.

[75] *AAS,* XLII (1950), 448. Cf. *infra,* p. 106.

torian of the sacrament of Orders, summarize the testimony of the past.

> The modern Roman Pontifical contains all that was found in earlier Pontificals, but the early Pontificals did not contain all that is found in the modern Roman Pontifical. For various motives of piety and religion led to the introduction into recent Pontificals of certain recent additions which were absent in all the earlier editions, and the later the date of these Pontificals, the more numerous the additions. But it is a remarkable and striking fact that in all these books, whether ancient, more modern, or contemporary, *there is one single form of ordination, both as concerns words and ceremonies, and the later books omit nothing of what was in the early ones. Thus the modern form of ordination differs not at all, whether in word or in rite, from that used by the ancient Fathers.*[76]

[76] *De Sacris Ordinationibus,* III, 10.—Quoted and translated by Messenger, *The Reformation, The Mass and the Priesthood* (2 vols., London–New York–Toronto: Longmans, Green and Co., 1936-1937), I, 61.

CHAPTER 2

THE GENERAL OBLIGATION OF OBSERVING THE RITES

ARTICLE I. FROM LITURGICAL LAW

As has been seen from the foregoing chapter, the laws governing the rites and ceremonies of sacred ordination prior to the sixteenth century were for the most part customary in their character. A certain autonomy was allowed the bishop as the minister of sacred Orders. The substance of the rites was duly guarded in consequence of the reverence for tradition as fostered by timely admonitions from the Holy See.[1] The fourteenth century, however, marked the beginning of a period of grave liturgical decline, in which the multiplication of rites and the numerous additions to the liturgy threatened the good order of public worship.[2]

This tendency was curbed only in consequence of the counter-reformation and reorganization initiated at the Council of Trent. This great reforming council reasserted the binding force of the "received and approved" rites for the administration of the sacraments,[3] and, what is more important, made a plea for new and authentic versions of the liturgical books.[4] The work was taken up immediately. During the pontificates of Pius IV (1559-1564) and Pius V (1566-1572) authentic editions of the Roman Breviary [5] and of the Roman Missal [6] were made of obligation for the

[1] Cf. Oppenheim, *Tractatus de Iure Liturgico,* Pars I, pp. 64-68.

[2] Jungmann, *The Mass of the Roman Rite: Its Origins and Development,* I, 173-177.

[3] Sessio VII, *Decretum de sacramentis, canones de sacramentis in genere,* Can. 13—Schroeder, *op. cit.,* pp. 53, 331.

[4] Sessio XXV, *Continuatio Sessionis, De Indice Librorum et Catechismo, Breviario et Missali*—Schroeder, *op. cit.,* pp. 254-255, 519-520.

[5] Pius V, litt. ap. *Quod a Nobis,* 9 iul. 1568—*Bullarum Diplomatum et Privilegiorum Romanorum Pontificum Taurinensis Editio* (24 vols. et Ap-

Western Church. On February 10, 1596, Pope Clement VIII (1592-1605) provided the Church with the first official and typical edition of the Roman Pontifical.[7]

In promulgating the Roman Pontifical the pope made very clear the legal force of the rites contained therein. He stated in his Constitution that thenceforth only these formulas were to be received and observed in all churches of the Latin Rite without exception, and continued:

> Decreeing that the aforesaid Pontifical must at no time be changed in whole or in part, or have anything added to or taken away from it, and that whosoever must exercise the pontifical functions, or otherwise must do or execute the matters that receive mention in the aforesaid Pontifical, are held to their performance and execution by the prescript and directive of this Pontifical, and that no one on whom the duty of exercising and doing these things has been imposed can satisfy this obligation of the law apart from the observance of the formulas which are contained in this Pontifical.[8]

Through this Constitution the traditional obligation of the minister with regard to the rites and ceremonies of sacred ordination passed into written law.

Vigilance for the observance of the sacred rites together with the solution of difficulties in their interpretation was originally placed within the competence of the *Congregatio pro Sacris Riti-*

---

pendix, Augustae Taurinorum, 1857-1872), VII, 685-688 (hereafter cited *BRT*).

6 Pius V, litt. ap. *Quo primum tempore,* 14 iul. 1570—*BRT,* VII, 839-841.

7 Const. *Ex quo in Ecclesia Dei—Codicis Iuris Canonici Fontes,* cura Em̃i Card. Gasparri Editi (9 vols., Romae: Typis Polyglottis Vaticanis, 1923-1939; Vols. VII-IX, ed. cura et studio Em̃i Iustiniani Card. Serédi), n. 180 (hereafter cited *Fontes*).

8 § 6: "Statuentes Pontificale praedictum nullo umquam tempore, in toto, vel in parte mutandum, vel ei aliquid addendum, aut omnino detrahendum esse, ac quoscumque, qui Pontificalia munera exercere, vel alias, quae in dicto Pontificali continentur, facere, aut exequi debent, ad ea peragenda, et praestanda, ex huius Pontificalis praescripto, et ratione teneri, neminemque ex iis, quibus ea exercendi, et faciendi munus impositum est, nisi formulis, quae hoc ipse Pontificali continentur servatis, satisfacere posse."—*Fontes,* n. 180.

bus et Caeremoniis.[9] The present *Congregatio Sacrorum Rituum*[10] retains this disciplinary function,[11] and thus the decrees of this Congregation are obligatory norms having the full force of law.[12] The general decrees, in accordance with the current normal rule, begin to bind upon the completion of three months from the date that appears on the fascicle of the *Acta Apostolicae Sedis* in which the pertinent text is included.[13] It was also common in the past to promulgate decrees of the Congregation by means of periodically issued authentic collections.[14] Particular decrees or responses, of course, bind only those to whom they are addressed, unless they become equivalently general. In this case they would bind universally.

While all the rubrics governing the rites are preceptive and bind in conscience, not all bind in the same degree. Authors generally distinguish between rubrics which are essential or substantial and those which are accidental or ceremonial.[15] The former pertain to the essence of the rite and govern actions and words which affect the validity of the liturgical action; the latter regulate ceremonies introduced by the Church, which are generally required not for the validity of the action, but simply for its lawfulness. It is evident that the essential rubrics bind gravely. In the past it has been easier to establish the existence of this rule

[9] Founded by Pope Sixtus V in January of the year 1588 with the promulgation of the bull *Immensa aeterni Dei.*—*BRT,* VIII, 989.

[10] Reformed by Pope Pius X in the reorganization of the Roman Curia detailed in his Apostolic Constitution *Sapienti consilio,* promulgated June 29, 1908.—*AAS,* I (1909), 7-58; *Fontes,* n. 682.

[11] Canon 253. The Congregation for the Discipline of the Sacraments retains jurisdiction where the validity of Orders is touched upon.—Canon 249, § 3.

[12] McManus, *The Congregation of Sacred Rites* (The Catholic University of American Canon Law Series, n. 352, Washington, D. C.: The Catholic University of America Press, 1954), p. 134.

[13] Canon 9.

[14] McManus, *op. cit.,* p. 135.

[15] Noldin-Schmitt, *Summa Theologiae Moralis* (26. ed., 3 vols., Oeniponte, Lipsiae: Rauch, 1940-1941), Vol. III, *De Sacramentis,* n. 31.

than to particularize its import because of the uncertainty as to what were the essential rites of sacred ordination. The Apostolic Constitution *Sacramentum Ordinis,* in establishing the matter and form of the Order of the episcopate, of the priesthood, and of the diaconate, leaves no room for doubt concerning the essential rites by which these Orders are conferred.

ARTICLE II. FROM THE CODE OF CANON LAW

In canon 1002 the Code of Canon Law takes to itself the full force of these liturgical laws and makes them its own in commanding that—

> The minister, in conferring any of the Orders, must observe the proper rites described in the Roman Pontifical and other liturgical books, which for no reason may be changed or inverted.[16]

It is clear than no new obligation is imposed through this canon, nor is any change made in the existing liturgical laws regarding the minister of Orders. The purpose of the law can be more clearly seen if some knowledge of the history of this canon is brought to light.

It is possible to obtain some indication of the mind of the legislator from a partial view of the *Acta Praeparatoria* of the Apostolic Commission entrusted with the task of drawing up the Code. Father Hürth by special permission was allowed to view the *Acta* while preparing a commentary on the Apostolic Constitution *Sacramentum Ordinis.*[17] He reveals that the Commission wished to include in the Code a canon treating of the repetition of the rites and the supplying for the defects in sacred ordination. To this end there was prepared a lengthy canon which outlined in detail what was to be done when the rites which were considered essential to the ordination were omitted or only doubtfully ap-

[16] "In quovis conferendo ordine, minister proprios ritus in Pontificali Romano aliisve ritualibus libris ab Ecclesia probatis descriptos, adamussim servet, quos nulla ratione licet praeterire vel invertere."

[17] Hürth, "Commentarium ad Constitutionem Apostolicam," *Periodica de Re Morali, Canonica, Liturgica* (Brugis, 1927-1936; Romae, 1937-), XXXVII (1948), 9-39 (hereafter cited *Periodica*).

plied. The first redaction of this canon was rejected by the members of the Commission, and another was proposed. The second version read:

> Si in sacra ordinatione quid essentiale omissum fuerit vel modo dubio positum, integra ordinatio iteretur absolute vel sub condictione.[18]

There was also much objection to this proposal, for here again the canon would be useless unless the *quid essentiale* were specifically known. Because of a lack of this certainty it was decided to remand the whole question concerning the essential rites of sacred ordination to the Sacred Congregation of the Holy Office for an authoritative decision. There the matter rested. As long, however, as the question remained in doubt, the only safe course which remained was to insist upon the faithful execution of all the rites and ceremonies of ordination to preclude any possibility of invalidity—or scruples to that effect by the ones receiving the Orders. Accordingly there was restated the grave obligation of the minister of Orders to follow in every detail the rites described in the approved liturgical books.

In enumerating the liturgical books to be followed, the canon, in addition to mentioning the Roman Pontifical, points also to other liturgical books approved by the Church. Inasmuch as the Code of Canon Law does not ordinarily legislate for the Oriental Churches unless they are specifically mentioned,[19] it may be presumed that the *Euchologium Graecorum* and other approved books for the Eastern Church are not designated here. Reference is probably made here to the approved rituals of certain religious orders which contain proper rites for the elevation of their subjects to minor Orders,[20] or other approved liturgical books of the non-Roman Western Rites as, for example, the *Pontificale* of the Ambrosian Rite. In any event the minister must always follow his proper rite when conferring Orders. The Holy See sometimes grants an indult for ordaining a candidate of another

[18] *Ibid.*, p. 10.

[19] Canon 1.

[20] E.g., *ordinarius seu Liber Caeremoniarum ad Usum Sacri et Canonici Ordinis Praemonstratensis* (Typis Abbatiae B.V.M. de Tongerloo, 1949), nn. 320-327.

rite in a ceremony not proper to his rite;[21] rarely is the opposite granted, however, whereby the minister ordains in a rite other than his own.

The final clause of the canon asserts that no reason will warrant the minister's omission or inversion of the prescribed rites. The minister is gravely bound to follow this provision, not only for certifying the validity of the Orders received, but also for insuring its lawful conferral through the use of all the words and actions by which the transfer of power is symbolized. Under ordinary circumstances any notable deviation would be gravely sinful. The law is not so inflexible, however, as to bind under the most grave and extraordinary circumstances. Cappello submits the opinion that this obligation would not bind in time of persecution or grave public calamity, when the full rites of ordination could not be performed without danger of grave harm to the principals involved or to the Church.[22] The validity of the ordination would have to be safeguarded, but here the minister would have the firm principles of the Apostolic Constitution *Sacramentum Ordinis* to rely upon. In accordance with the past practice of the Church, which will be seen more fully in the following chapter, the minister would be obliged to supply the omitted rites, but this he could undertake also out of season and apart from all publicity.[23]

[21] Canon 1004.

[22] *Tractatus Canonico-Moralis de Sacramentis* (5 vols., Vol. IV, *De Sacra Ordinatione,* 3. ed., Romae, 1951), IV, n. 563 (hereafter cited *De Sacra Ordinatione*).

[23] Canon 1007.

CHAPTER 3

THE REPAIR OF DEFECTIVE RITES PRIOR TO THE APOSTOLIC CONSTITUTION *SACRAMENTUM ORDINIS*

Consideration must now be given to the secondary obligation of the ordaining minister, by which he is held to repair the rites when an Order has been defectively conferred. With the many ordinations in the Church it is inevitable that through error or inadvertence the general obligation of performing all the rites and ceremonies prescribed by the Church has not been faithfully observed. The defective rites that have resulted have been the cause of many doubts concerning the lawfulness or even the validity of the Orders received. This was especially true before the pronouncement of Pius XII concerning the essential matter and form of the sacrament of Orders, and, as will be seen, was the reason why the Holy Father felt the need to speak on the subject.

This fact suggests the division of this matter into a review of the practice of the Church developed prior to the Apostolic Constitution *Sacramentum Ordinis* and a consideration of the repair of defective rites after the provisions of the Constitution attained the force of law. The former division, presented in this chapter, will attempt to trace the history and development of this practice during the centuries when the Church was not guided by an official pronouncement concerning the essential rites of sacred ordination.

Article I. A Practice Developing

The popes and ecclesiastical writers prior to the twelfth century did not treat specifically of the procedure that was to be followed when a mistake or some omission had occurred in the conferring of Orders. The ordination ceremony was looked upon as a whole, and the sum of all the individual rites was jealously guarded. As the ordination ceremony became invested with a more fixed form, however, the various parts of the whole commanded more attention, and their relative importance to the sacrament conferred became a subject of controversy. Papal responses recorded in the *Corpus Iuris Canonici* present the basis from which this controversy grew.

A. *The* Decretum *of Gratian*

Gratian († ca. 1157) presented but one case of defective rite. A bishop, because of poor eyesight, allowed an assisting priest to read the consecratory prayer while he (the bishop) imposed hands in the ordination of one priest and two lectors. The bishop and priest were declared deserving of punishment for acting against the accustomed order of the Church.[1] As for the ones so ordained: *"Hi, qui supersunt, gradum sacerdotii vel levitici ordinis, quem perverse adepti sunt, amittant."* [2]

No mention is made of the repair of the defective rite. The glossator failed to offer any helpful commentary on this point, but he did state that not all mistakes or acts of neglect in the ceremony of ordination have an invalidating force. Certain solemnities could be separated from the personal action of the ordaining bishop, inasmuch as this did not pertain to the very substance of the ordination. Unfortunately the glossator failed to specify the acts that fell into that category.[3]

Elsewhere in the *Decretum*, Gratian treated specifically of the problem of doubtful ordination. The chaper *Presbyteri* under Distinction LXVIII presented the response of Pope Gregory I (540-604) to the Archbishop of Ravenna, in answer to a ques-

[1] "Et ordinator, et ordinatus damnationis subeat poenam, cum episcopus manum imponit, et alius orationem dicit. Quorundam clericorum dum unus ad presbyterium, duo ad levitarum ministerium sacrarentur, episcopus oculorum dolore detentus, fertur super eos manum suam tantum imposuisse, et presbyter quidam illis contra ecclesiasticum ordinem benedictionem dedisse."—C. 14, D. XXIII.

[2] The origin of this canon is doubtful. Gratian referred it to a Toledan Council. The *Palea* of c. 13, D. XXIII, presented a very similar case as a reply of Pope Severinus († 640). The origin of both is most probably found in a letter of Pope Simplicius (468-483) to the Florentine bishops in 474 (JK, n. 339). The same case receives mention in the fifth canon of the Council of Seville (619).—Mansi, X, 558.

[3] *Glossa Ordinaria,* s.v. *amittant,* ad c. 14, D. XXIII.

tion concerning the validity of ordinations conferred by one who himself was doubtfully a bishop. The archbishop asked whether, in the face of a prohibition against reordination, these ordinations should or should not be repeated. Gregory answered that, if the men so ordained were worthy and fit subjects for the priesthood, they were to receive again the sacerdotal unction from their own bishops, and only then were they to enter upon the sacred ministry.[4]

This reply clarified for Gratian the status of the doubtfully ordained. Their reordination did not offend against the strict prohibition against repeating a sacrament which imprinted an indelible character.[5] The glossator added that in the matter of doubtful ordination it was more safe to presume that one was not ordained than to presume the ordination to be valid.[6] This principle was to become the first rule in all cases of doubtful ordination. The safeguarding of the validity of the sacrament of Orders demanded that such a cautious course be followed.

B. *The Decretals of Gregory IX*

Defects in the rites of sacred ordination are treated under two titles in the Decretals of Gregory IX: *De sacra unctione* and *De sacramentis non iterandis.* Their enumeration under the latter title suggests that St. Raymond of Peñafort († 1275), the illustrious Spanish Dominican who compiled the Decretals for Pope Gregory, was aware of the above mentioned principle of Gratian. The commentary he offered will be presented along with the chapters as they are treated. Three cases of defective rites are delineated in the Decretals. In each case the repair of the rite is sought through the command of supplying that which had been lacking or which had been defectively done.

The first such instance is found in the Decretal *Cum venisset.* It reproduces a letter which Pope Innocent III (1198-1216) had directed to the Primate of the Bulgarians.[7] It had come to the

[4] C. 2, D. LXVIII.

[5] *Dictum Gratiani,* ad c. 2, D. LXVIII.

[6] *Glossa Ordinaria,* s.v. *consecrentur.*

[7] C. 1, X, *De sacra unctione,* 1, 15; Potthast, *Regesta Pontificum Romanorum inde ab anno post Christum natum 1198 ad annum 1304* (2 vols.,

attention of the Pope that a Greek bishop had been consecrated in Rome without the anointing of the head and hands with chrism, as was the custom in the Roman Church. Innocent III took this occasion to instruct the bishops of the East on the necessity of anointing in the consecration of a bishop, in the ordination of a priest and in the administration of the sacrament of confirmation. He prefaced his letter with the command that the anointings which had been omitted in the consecration of the Greek bishop had to be supplied.[8]

The glossator interpreted this command as an admonition to the whole Church that the custom of the Apostolic See establishes a norm in these matters which must be observed, but he advanced no opinion as to whether this consecration, without the use of chrism, was considered valid or merely unlawful.[9] Perhaps he did not consider such a pronouncement necessary, for consecration without the use of oil for anointing had always been accepted as valid in the Eastern Church. This ceremony, in that event, was only an accidental part of the rite, which by command of Pope Innocent was to be considered as necessary for the solemnity of episcopal consecration.

St. Raymond of Peñafort held this opinion. In his commentary on the Decretals he stated that the omission of the unction did not vitiate that which has been done.[10] He argued that when the law commands only a supplying for the defect rather than a repetition of the whole rite, this judgment could always be made. When an ordination or a consecration was substantially defective or even doubtfully so, he demanded the repetition of the entire consecration, for in such an eventuality the whole rite

---

Berolini, 1874-1875), n. 2138—dated 1204 (hereafter cited Potthast); *MPL*, CCXV, 282.

[8] C. 1, X, *De sacra unctione*, 1, 15. Pope Innocent III referred to the practice of anointing as of Apostolic origin. He cited as authority, however, a false letter ascribed to Pope Anacletus in the pseudo-Isidorian Decretals. Cf. Hinchius, *Decretales Pseudo-Isidorianae* (Lipsiae, 1863), p. 75; Ellard, *Ordination Anointing in the Western Church before 1000 A.D.*, pp. 31-50.

[9] *Glossa Ordinaria*, s.v. *monemus*.

[10] ". . . quod etiam si unctio amissa fuerit non vitiatur quod factum est." —*Summa Aurea* (Romae, 1603), Lib. III, Tit. 22, n. 11.

was vitiated and nothing was effected.[11] If, on the other hand, something was omitted which was expressly not of the substance of the rite, then, so St. Raymond stated, the ordination or consecration was not to be repeated, but that which was incautiously omitted was to be cautiously supplied.[12]

Panormitanus (Nicholaus de Tudeschis, † 1453),[13] Cardinal Hostiensis (Henricus de Segusio, † 1271),[14] and others in treating of the repair of a defective rite in the conferral of Orders did little more than quote St. Raymond. They referred to the ceremonies which must be supplied as necessary solemnities as distinguished from unnecessary solemnities, which as neither grave nor dishonorable ommissions did not need to be supplied.

A second letter of Innocent II called for the repair of a defective rite by means of an act that supplied for the defect. In the Decretal *Pastoralis* the imposition of hands which had been omitted in the ordination of a subdeacon was ordered to be supplied.[15]

This occasioned some difficulty for the glossator, for he was aware of the prohibition against the imposition of hands in the ordination of subdeacons as found in all the Sacramentaries and Pontificals. He could only conclude that the phrase "imposition of hands" implied some blessing at the end of the ceremony.[16] Pope Innocent IV (Sinibaldus Fliscus), writing as a private canonist, referred to this gloss as unnecessary, and revealed that the original letter contained the word *diaconus,* rather than *subdiaconus.*[17]

This seemed to defeat the distinction made by St. Raymond.

[11] *Loc. cit.*

[12] "Quod non est de substantia, non debet ordinatio, nec consecratio, iterari; sed quod omissus est debet caute suppleri statuto tempore . ." —*Loc. cit.*

[13] *Commentaria in Quinque Libros Decretalium* (5 vols., in 7, Venetiis, 1588), Lib. I, Tit. II, n. 2, ad c. 1, X, *De sacra unctione,* 1, 15.

[14] *Commentaria in Quinque Libros Decretalium* (5 vols., Venetiis, 1581), Lib. 1, Tit. XIV, c. 1.

[15] C. 1, X, *De sacramentis non iterandis,* 1, 16; The original letter is also to be found in *MPL,* CCXV, 428; Potthast, n. 2350.

[16] *Glossa Ordinaria,* s.v. *impositione.*

[17] *Commentaria super Decretales* (Venetiis, 1570), Lib. 1, Tit. XVI, c. 1.

Innocent IV, however, since he also held that the imposition of hands was of the substance of the rite for the diaconate, interpreted the *supplendum* to imply a virtual repetition of the ordination with only certain solemnities omitted.[18] He did not specify what these solemnities included, however.

The final Decretal occasioned much difficulty among theologians and canonists in their discussions concerning the essential rite of the sacrament of Orders.[19] It reads:

> Presbyter et diaconus cum ordinatur, manus impositionem tactu corporali (ritu ab Apostolis introducto) recipiunt. Quod si omissum fuerit, non est aliquatenus iterandum, sed statuto tempore ad huiusmodi ordines conferendos caute supplendum quod per errorem exstitit praetermissum. Suspensio autem manuum debet fieri, cum oratio super caput effunditur ordinandi.[20]

The glossator was explicit in stating that only the imposition of hands by way of physical touch was to be supplied for the repairing of the defect mentioned in the Decretal.[21] Although the rite was introduced by the Apostles, so he continued, this did not preclude the possibility of its institution by Christ.[22] Did the glossator suggest here that the imposition of hands by way of physical touch, even though it was essential to the rite of ordination through Christ's institution, was alone to be supplied? If so, no author after him followed his opinion. Many (1847-1922), however, did point to the phrase *ab Apostolis introducto* and the simple supplying of the rite called for in the Decretal as proof that the imposition of hands was not an essential rite in the ordination of priests and deacons.[23]

18 "Sed quasi totum iterandum nisi forte propter aliquas solemnitates, quae non reiterabantur si primo factae fuerunt."—*Loc. cit.*

19 Cf. Cappello, *De Sacra Ordinatione*, n. 118.

20 C. 3, X, *De sacramentis non iterandis*, 1, 16; Potthast, n. 9056. The original letter was written by Gregory IX (1227-1234) to the Bishop of London.

21 *Glossa Ordinaria*, s.v. *presbyter*.

22 *Glossa Ordinaria*, s.v. *ritu;* Innocent IV, Gonzalez, Pirhing, and others followed this explanation according to Cappello, *op. cit.*, n. 162, p. 118.

23 *Infra*, pp. 38-39.

St. Raymond of Peñafort, who was in a better position to know the mind of Gregory IX than others, offered the best explanation of the Decretal. He characterized the defect as one of only necessary solemnity, and not as one of the substance of the rite.[24] He accepted the imposition of hands in the ordination of a priest or of a deacon as the essential rite of ordination, but indicated that the required *tactus corporalis* added a new element that could not be so considered. This opinion is vindicated in the Constitution *Sacramentum Ordinis,* where Pius XII (1939-1958) commanded that the imposition of hands be accomplished by means of a physical touching of the head of the person to be ordained, but added that a moral contact is sufficient for the valid conferring of the sacrament.[25]

The few glossators and decretalists who treated of the rites of ordination evidenced a caution that was understandable in attempting to expand upon the substantive law found in the decretals. The fundamental importance of the sacrament of Orders and the lack of authoritative interpretation from the Holy See contributed to their hesitance. Norms were gradually being developed, however, for the evaluation and the repair of the defects occurring in the rites of ordination. The following principles formed the basis for the accepted usage which evolved.

1. The sacrament of Orders, when validly conferred, was never to be repeated.

2. If there was omitted a part of the rite which the canons established as substantial to the rite, nothing was effected, and therefore the whole ordination was to be repeated.

3. A defect was presumed to be of the substance of the rite, unless the contrary was clearly expressed in the law.

4. If the omitted factors were expressly not of the substance of the rite, then there was no need for a repetition of the entire rite, but there was to be a supplying simply for the defect itself.

5. Certain light omissions and mistakes were so inconsequential that there was no need at all of supplying for them.

Having advanced this far, the canonists could go no further. Where exactly were the esssential rites of the various Orders to

24 *Summa Aurea,* Lib. III, Tit. 22, n. 11.

25 *AAS,* XL (1948), p. 7, n. 6.

be found? What words and actions were absolutely necessary for the substance of the sacrament? What of the intention of the minister? In doubt whether some omitted prayer or action was of the substance of the sacrament or not, should the whole ordination be repeated, or only a part? [26] These were questions that had to be answered. Consideration will now be given to the efforts of the canonists and theologians to meet this need.

Article II. Opinions concerning the Essential Rites of Sacred Ordination

The development of the rites and ceremonies of ordination from the simple laying on of hands to the elaborate Romano-Germanic ritual made obscure the exact moment when the sacramental sign was complete. No action or precise formula of words could be singled out, as could be done, for example, in the sacrament of baptism, as the exclusive rite by which the character of Orders was imprinted. The question was, therefore, open to speculation. The opinions that developed were as varied and diverse as the rites themselves.

Historically the Order of the priesthood was the center of discussion. This was due largely to the fact that the early scholastics treated the question in their commentary on the chapter *De presbyteris* in the Sentences of Peter Lombard.[27] The same restriction of the subject will be followed here. The arguments presented for the essential rite in the ordination of priests can be easily accommodated to the other sacramental Orders. The subdiaconate will not be discussed. Since it was an institution of comparatively recent foundation, few questioned the right of the Church to designate or even to change the essential rite by which it was conferred.

A. *Opinions of the Thirteenth and Fourteenth Centuries*

The *Sentences* of Peter Lombard (1100-1160) may be said to mark the transition from an expository treatment of the sacrament of Orders to a more scientific examination of its various

[26] Cf. Guido de Baysio, *Rosarium super Decreto* (Venetiis, 1577), C. VIII, D. XXIII, s.v. *Episcopus.*

[27] Lib. IV, D. XXIV, cap. XI.

parts. With reference to the essential rites of ordination, Peter Lombard was satisfied with merely compiling the opinions of Gratian (d. ca. 1157), of Hugh of St. Victor († 1141), and of Ivo of Chartres († 1117).[28] Those who in turn commented upon the *Sentences* came to grips with the question.

St. Bonaventure (1221-1274) was the first explicitly to ask: At what part of the ceremony is the sacramental character imprinted?[29] In answering this question he sought to determine that external sign and formula or words which, in the ordination of a priest, signified the principal power conferred. He concluded that the character is impressed at the imposition of hands by the bishop. Two arguments especially led him to this conclusion. The hands constituted a man's instruments *par excellence* (*organum organorum*); therefore it was fitting that the power and character of sacerdotal Orders be transferred by this means rather than through some lesser instrument such as the chalice, the book, the keys, etc., as used in the conferring of minor Orders. He seemed more convinced, however, by the argument from history. The Scriptures did not record the use of any instrument other than the hands in the Apostolic Church.[30]

Using the same premise, St. Thomas (1225-1274) arrived at a different conclusion. Viewing the ceremony from the aspect of the priestly powers conferred, he found the principal act of the priest to be the consecration of the bread and the wine. Thus the character was conferred at the moment when this principal power was signified by the *traditio* of the chalice and the paten. Looking at the ordination as a whole (he must have used some version of the Romano-Germanic Pontifical with the ceremonies grouped together after the tract), he distinguished two principal actions: The preparation for the reception of Orders and the actual ordination. The litany, the anointings and the delivery of the vestments all were acts of preparation, as was also the im-

[28] Lib. IV, D. XXIV, cap. XI. These three writers seemed to hold that the anointing was the essential rite of ordination.

[29] *In IV Sent.* (ca. 1248), D. 24, 2, a. 1, q. 4.

[30] It is certain that Bonaventura referred to the first imposition of hands, for the final imposition of hands had not been introduced into the ceremony when he wrote (ca. 1248).

position of hands by which the fullness of grace was received. Only afterwards was the character received with the delivery of the chalice and the paten, the essential rite in the conferral of priestly Orders.[31]

John Duns Scotus (1266-1308), writing after the ceremony had reached its full development as exemplified in the Pontifical of Durantis, noted that the *traditio* was held to be the matter of the sacrament of Orders in the Western Church, while the imposition of hands was so considered in the Churches of the East. Both of these rites, he granted, could be used to signify the power received, but it seemed more probable that both should be considered as partial matter for the sacrament, the first to signify the power of the priest over the physical body of Christ in the act of consecration, and the second to signify the power over the mystical body in the act of absolution. Scotus had a twofold answer for the question proposed by Bonaventure. The essential rites for the conferring of the power of the priesthood were the delivery of the chalice and the paten along with the *last* imposition of hands.[32] This explanation fitted perfectly the advanced development of the rite of ordination[33] and the gospel account of Our Lord's actions with reference to the Apostles.

The opinions of St. Bonaventure, St. Thomas, and Duns Scotus, separately and in various combinations, continued to be held through the fifteenth century, with none, except that of St. Thomas, commanding such a following that it could warrantably have been regarded as the common opinion of theologians or canonists in any given period.

B. *The Decree for the Armenians*

In the midst of this controversy, the first official pronouncement by the Church concerning the essential matter and form of the sacrament of Orders was issued on November 22, 1439, by Pope Eugene IV (1431-1447), in a decree addressed to the Armenian Church. In the sixth section of this document the following statement was made concerning the sacrament of Orders:

31 *In IV Sent.*, D. 24, q. 2, a. 3.

32 *In IV Sent.*, D. 24, q. 1, a. 3.

33 Bligh, *Ordination to the Priesthood*, p. 45.

> Sextum sacramentum est *Ordinis*, cuius materia est illud, per cuius traditionem confertur ordo: sicut presbyteratus traditur per calicis cum vino et patenae cum pane porrectionem. Diaconatus vero per libri Evangeliorum dationem. Subdiaconatus vero per calicis vacui cum patena vacua superposita traditionem: . . . Forma sacerdotali talis est: *Accipe potestatem offerendi sacrificium in ecclesia pro vivis et mortuis, in nomine Patris et Filii et Spiritus Sancti.* Et sic de aliorum ordinum formis, prout in Pontificali Romano late continetur.[34]

This was exactly the doctrine of St. Thomas; in fact, it was taken, for the most part, from a treatise of his written at the request of the Archbishop of Palermo.[35] Strangely enough this pronouncement left the European controversy comparatively untouched until the following century. The Chancellor of Louvain, Ruard Tapper (1487-1599), was the first to claim the pronouncement of the Council of Florence to be *de fide* in support of his argument that the *traditio instrumentorum,* beyond all doubt, constituted the essential rite of the sacrament of Orders.[36] Others,[37] following the opinion of St. Thomas, used this decree together with the Decretal of Pope Gregory IX mentioned above [38] to vindicate their position.

Not all authors, however, considered the decree to have such

[34] *Enchiridion,* n. 701. This famous *Decretum pro Armenis* was ratified in a solemn session of the Ecumenical Council of Florence as reflecting " . . *quodam brevi compendio orthodoxae fidei veritatem*" and signed by Pope Eugene IV, eight cardinals, two patriarchs, five archbishops, thirty-five bishops, twenty-five abbots and the Armenian envoys.—Hofmann, *Documenta Concilii Florentini de Unione Orientalium,* II, *De Unione Armenorum,* Textus et Documenta, Series Theologica, n. 19 (Romae: Universitas Gregoriana, 1935), pp. 44-45.

[35] *S. Thomas Opera Omnia* (25 vols., Parmae: Fiaccodori, 1852-1873), Vol. XVI, Opusc. IV, *In Articulos Fidei et Sacramentorum Ecclesiae Expositio,* p. 121.

[36] *Opera* (3 vols., Romae, 1599), Vol. II, art. XVII, *De Sacramento Ordinis.*

[37] Candidus (1572-1654), Angles († 1587) and Gonet (1616-1681)—Van Rossum, *De Essentia Sacramenti Ordinis* (Editio altera, Romae: Fridericus Pustet, 1931), p. 18.

[38] *Supra,* pp. 31-32.

force. St. Alphonsus (1696-1787) [39] and Pope Benedict XIV (Prospero Lambertini [1675-1758]) [40] were of the opinion that Eugene IV did not intend to determine the essential matter of the sacrament, but desired simply to present a practical instruction to the Armenian Church concerning the use of the delivery of the instruments, and in no way sought to settle the question. This opinion presumes that the Armenians were in ignorance of the use of the *traditio instrumentorum* in the West. There is good evidence to show, however, that the use of the chalice and the paten in the ordination ceremony had been the custom in the Armenian Church for two hundred years before the decree was issued. In a reply to this specific question proposed by Pope Benedict XII (1334-1342), the Armenians, gathered at Sis in 1344, sent to Rome a Latin translation of their ordination ceremony, which did include the delivery of the paten and the chalice.[41]

Among the modern authors this sharp difference of opinion continued. Gasparri (1852-1934) termed the decree doctrinal, but neither definitive nor infallible.[42] Cardinal Van Rossum (1854-1932) took the extreme view that the decree contained doctrinal error.[43] De Guibert (1877-1942),[44] P. Galtier (1872-),[45] Billot

[39] *Theologia Moralis* (ed. nova, cura L. Gaudé, 7 libri in 4 vols., Romae: Typis Polyglottis Vaticanis, 1905-1912), Tom. III, Lib. VI, n. 12.

[40] *De Synodo Dioecesana* (2. ed., 2 vols., Parmae, 1764), Lib. VIII, Cap. X, n. 8. The Pope here was writing as a private theologian.

[41] *Concilium Armenorum,* c. 92—Mansi, XXV, 1260.

[42] *Tractatus Canonicus de Sacra Ordinatione* (2 vols., Parisiis, 1893), I, n. 1007.

[43] *De Essentia Sacramenti Ordinis,* pp. 182-197. This opinion is consistent with his view that the matter and the form of the sacrament and the substance of the sacrament are identifiable concepts. Thus, the Church, which admittedly has no power over the substance of the sacrament, could not change its matter and form.

[44] "Le Décret du Concile de Florence pour les Arméniens, sa valeur dogmatique," *Bulletin de Littérature Ecclésiastique,* X (1919), 81-95, 150-216.

[45] "Imposition des mains," *Dictionnaire de Théologie Catholique* (Paris, 1903-), VII, 1411.

(1846-1931) [46] and others defended the full conciliar authority of the *Decretum pro Armenis* and concluded that the Pope effected a change in the matter and the form of the sacrament of Orders. Their arguments, upholding the power of the Church to change the essential rites of the sacrament of Orders, or the matter and the form of this sacrament, are convincing. They do not, however, explain the action of the Council with regard to the Greek Church as taken a little before the Armenian envoys arrived, nor the lack of insistence that this conciliar decree settled the matter once for all. Another author proposed the opinion that the decree was intended by the Council to constitute the *traditio instrumentorum* as the essential matter in the Armenian Church only.[47]

There is no question of papal infallibility. Pope Eugene IV, in issuing the decree, was acting not as shepherd and teacher of all Christians, but only as teacher of the Armenian Church to whom the decree was addressed. The most weighty argument against the binding force of the *Decretum pro Armenis* was the continuation of the controversy in the West. Certainly the writers before, during and after the Council of Trent did not consider the matter closed.

C. *The Council of Trent and Beyond*

Opinion before the Council of Trent leaned heavily to the side of St. Thomas. To Dominic Soto (1494-1560) the contention that the *sola traditio instrumentorum* was essential became a simple conclusion drawn from the Council of Florence. He went so far as to say that this was the common opinion of his day.[48]

The renewal of interest in the scriptural illustration of the beginnings of the sacraments as a consequence of the so-called Protestant reformation, however, brought the simple Apostolic rite of the imposition of hands to prominence again. Men like

[46] *De Ecclesiae Sacramentis Commentarius in Tertiam partem S. Thomae* (2 vols., Vol. I, 7. ed., Romae, 1931; Vol. II, 9. ed., Romae, 1929), II, 273.

[47] Bligh, *Ordination to the Priesthood*, p. 53.

[48] "Haec est opinio communis a qua non est temere recedendum."—*In IV Sententiarum* (Venetiis, 1538), D. 24, q. 1, a. 4.

John Faber (1470-1530), Tillman Smeling (1515-1557) and Stanislaus Cardinal Hosius (1504-1579) [49] placed great emphasis on the imposition of hands as the external sign of grace in the sacrament of Orders. It is difficult to determine whether they also held that the power of Orders was so conferred. John Eck (1486-1543), the great opponent of Luther (1483-1546), went to great lengths to extol the Apostolic rite, but concluded:

> Est et haec sanctorum Patrum sententia . . . quod quamvis diaconorum et presbyterorum ordinatio in sacris litteris nomine impositionis manus exprimatur, tamen neque illorum ordinum substantialis pars est impositio manuum, cum sine ea possit ordinari presbyter, sicut Gregorius IX scribit.[50]

Alfonso de Castro (1495-1558), however, found the scriptural evidence convincing, and correspondingly concluded that the imposition of hands was the essential rite of priestly ordination.[51]

The emphasis on Scripture was also evidenced by the frequent reference to the formula "*Accipe Spiritum Sanctum. . . .*" Peter Soto (1495-1563) tended to the opinion that this formula with the last imposition of hands was the essential rite of ordination rather than the *traditio* of the chalice.[52] When confronted with the Decretal of Gregory IX, however, he thought it better to leave the question in doubt.[53]

Within the Council of Trent this uncertainty continued. Among the theologians present, Martin Pérez de Ayala (1504-1564), Bishop of Segovia, objected to the *traditio instrumentorum* because of the lack of scriptural proof for its use in the early Church. He argued:

49 Cf. Giovani Battista de Farnese, *Il Sacramento dell' Ordine nel periodo precedente la Sessione XXIII di Trento, 1515-1562* (Romae: Pontificia Universitas Gregoriana, 1946), pp. 234-256.

50 Eckius, *Homliae sive Sermones adversus Quoscumque Nostri Haereticos* (Coloniae, 1537), Hom. 54, p. 567.

51 "Primum ergo ostendere volo in collatione ordinis gratiam conferri, deinde ostendam ex sacris litteris huius rei esse—aliquod signum sensibile. E quibus duobus concludetur esse—Sacramentum."—*Adversus Omnes Haereses Libri XIV* (Parisiis, 1564), Lib. III, n. 201.

52 *Tractatus de Institutione Sacerdotum* (Dillingae, 1560), n. 279.

53 *Loc. cit.*

> Non placet mihi illud quod dicitur de traditione calicis in coena, quod fuerit symbolum ordinationis sacerdotalis, quo apostoli fuerunt ordinati a Christo, cum omnino sine ratione dicatur, nec auctoritate Scripturae neque sanctorum patrum fulciatur. Nec vidi umquam apud antiquos sanctos et doctores (modernam doctrinam excipio) ordinem presbyteratus conferri traditionem calicis huiusmodi solum, sed manuum impositionem praecipuam ceremoniam ordinis reputari ab eis, id quod sonant sacrae Litterae et concilium Carthaginense subindicat.[54]

Others [55] seemed to support the doctrine of St. Thomas, holding that Christ did not directly institute the matter and the form of the sacrament of Orders, and therefore tradition, and not Scripture, presented the course to be followed. At least one of the theologians held to the opinion of Scotus.[56]

The Fathers of the Council were very much aware of the conflicting views on this matter, as is evident from the revisions of the various schemata treating of the sacrament of Orders. One such redaction presented on the thirteenth of October, 1562, read:

> Iam vero, cum ex scripturae testimonio et ecclesiastica traditione satis perspicuum sit, ordinem externo signo sensibili administrari, potestatemque spiritualem et gratiam per id conferri: dubitare nemo potest, vere et proprie sacramentum dicendum esse. Huic enim pertinet, quod legimus, Dominum quidem apostolis calicem in coena tradidisse, post resurrectionem in eos insufflasse, apostolos autem postquam ieiunassent et orassent, iis, qui ordinandi erant, manus imposuisse, quorum exemplum deinceps sancta ecclesia secuta, in ordinum collatione solemnibus caeremoniis usa est, atque inter eas sacram unctionem religios semper servavit.[57]

[54] *Concilium Tridentium, Diariorum, Actorum, Epistularum, Tractatuum Nova Collectio* (ed. Societas Goerresiana, 13 vols., Friburgi Brisgoviae: Herder and Co., 1901-), Vol. IX, *Concilii Tridentini Actorum Collectio, Complectens Acta post Sessionem Sextam (XXII) usque ad Finem Concilii (17 Sept. 1562–4 Dec. 1563)*, p. 75 (hereafter cited *C. Tr.*).

[55] *Ibid.* (Cardinal Cristoforo Madruzzo [1512-1578]), p. 46; (Egidio Foscarari [1512-1564], Bishop of Modena) p. 79.

[56] The Franciscan theologian Antonio Battista of Brugnolo—*C. Tr.*, IX, 13-14.

[57] *C. Tr.*, IX, 39.

After three revisions, in which mention of the individual rites was specifically made and then omitted again, the final pronouncement of the Council was:

> Cum Scripturae testimonio, apostolica traditione et patrum unanimi consensu perspicuum sit, per sacram ordinationem, quae verbis et signis exterioribus perficitur, gratiam conferri, . . .[58]

Certainly the Fathers and theologians of the Council did not consider the pronouncement of the Council of Florence to have settled the matter of the essential rites of the major Orders. Nor do the acts of the Council give any evidence that would show that the question received definitive treatment in its hands. Two other canons do make mention of specific rites used in the ordination ceremony,[59] but only to condemn the opinions of heretics who claim their use to be unnecessary.[60]

After the Council of Trent the opinion of St. Thomas did not command the following of a great number of writers. Fagnanus (1598-1678) was among the few who held strictly to the *sola traditio instrumentorum* as the essential action in the conferring of Sacred Orders.[61] Most of the writers along with Bellarmine (1542-1621),[62] Hallier (1595-1659)[63] and others[64] adhered to the twofold matter of the sacrament, the *traditio* of the chalice and the paten and the last imposition of hands. This opinion fell into disfavor in the seventeenth and eighteenth centuries, when the printing of the early liturgical books by Morinus (1591-1659), Bona (1609-1674), Martène (1654-1739) and others brought to

[58] Con. Trident., Sessio XXIII, c. 3—*Enchiridion*, n. 959.

[59] Conc. Trident., Sessio XXIII, cc. 4, 5—*Enchiridion*, nn. 464, 465.

[60] *C. Tr.*, IX, 5.

[61] *Commentaria in Quinque Libros Decretalium* (4 vols., Venetiis, 1709), Lib. 1, Cap. III, n. 5.

[62] *Omnia Opera* (6 vols., Neapoli, 1856-1861), III, Lib. 1, Cap. IX, n. 2.

[63] *De Sacris Electionibus et Ordinationibus ex Antiquo et Novo Ecclesiae Usu* (2. ed., 3 vols., Romae, 1739), II, Pars 2, Art. 1, n. XIV.

[64] Sanchez (1550-1610), Reiffenstuel (1642-1703), Schmalzgrueber (1663-1735), etc.—Cappello, *De Sacra Ordinatione*, p. 120.

light the comparatively recent origin of these two rites.[65] The opinion of St. Bonaventure came to be the common, but not undisputed, opinion of theologians and canonists, always, however, with a cautious eye to the Council of Florence.[66] Thus, Benedict XIV advised all bishops to avoid making any local legislation with reference to defects in the rites of Sacred Orders; rather, they were to submit their questions to Rome and to the Sacred Congregations for a proper solution.[67] In the following article the answers to these questions will be examined.

Article III. The Responses of the Sacred Congregations

Doubts concerning the validity and the lawfulness of major Orders as arising from defects of rite were submitted to five Roman Congregations and a Roman Tribunal: The Congregation of the Council, the Congregation of Sacred Rites, the Congregation of the Sacraments, the Congregation for the Propagation of the Faith, the Congregation of the Holy Office, and the Sacred Penitentiary. A collection of their replies in relation to each of the Orders under discussion will present a view of what was considered a safe norm for acting prior to the Apostolic Constitution *Sacramentum Ordinis*,[68] which represents the first definitive expression of law with reference to the classification of the rites of sacred ordination.

A. *The Subdiaconate*

a) *Defects in Essential Rites*

The Order of the subdiaconate is conferred when the bishop delivers the empty chalice and paten to the ordinand while pronouncing the words: *Videte cuius ministerium vobis traditur; ideo vos admoneo, ut ita vos exhibeatis, ut Deo placere possitis.* When this rite is omitted or substantially changed, the whole ordination must be repeated. The rite is substantially defective if the bishop does not personally hand the instruments to the

[65] Bligh, *Ordination to the Priesthood,* p. 47.

[66] Cf. Alphonsus Liguori, *Theologia Moralis,* Lib. VI, n. 748.

[67] *De Synodo Dioecesana,* Lib. VIII, Cap. X.

[68] *AAS,* XL (1948), 5-7; also see Appendix II.

one to be ordained, or if the one to be ordained does not touch them.[69]

Two or three of the candidates may, however, touch the instruments at the same time.[70] It is apparent from the words of the Pontifical that the chalice and paten are to be offered and touched *per modum unius.*[71] Therefore, when the chalice is touched but not the paten, or vice versa, the ordination is valid, and no repair is necessary.[72] The same is true if the chalice contains wine, or if there is a host on the paten, or if the chalice which is used is unconsecreated.[73]

b) *Defects in Integral Rites*

When the Book of Epistles is not presented by the bishop, or touched by the one being ordained, the whole ordination need not be repeated, but this rite alone is to be supplied. This may be done at any time, even privately and outside Mass, provided only that the book is delivered while the bishop at the same time pronounces the formula or words found in the Pontifical.[74]

c) *Defects in Incidental Rites*

The delivery of the cruets, which are offered by the archdeacon and not by the bishop, is an incidental part of the rite and, if

69 S.C.C., 10 ian. 1711: "Si Ordinandus in suscipiendo subdiaconatu tetigit quidem calicem et patenam, non autem librum epistolarum, Episcopus defectum suppleat, etiam privatim."—Pallottini, *Collectio Omnium Conclusionum et Resolutionum S. Congregationis Concilii ad anno 1564 ad annum 1860* (17 vols., Romae, 1868-1893), XVI, p. 68, n. 4 (hereafter cited Pallottini).

70 Gasparri, *De Sacra Ordinatione,* II, nn. 1017, 1063.

71 "Deinde Pontifex accipit, et tradit omnibus Calicem vacuum, cum Patena vacua superposita, quem successive manu dextera singuli tangunt . . ."—*Pontificale Romanum,* Summorum Pontificum jussu editum, a Benedicto XIV et Leone XIII Pontificibus Maximis recognitum et castigatum (Mechliniae: Dessain, 1895), Tit. *De Ordinatione Subdiaconi.*

72 Many, *Praelectiones de Sacra Ordinatione,* n. 289, 2.

73 S.C.S. Off., 28 ian., 1937—A private response reported by F. X. Hecht († 1953) in the *Periodica,* XXVI (1937), 184.

74 S.R.C., *Taurinen.,* 16 iunii, 1873—*Decreta Authentica Congregationis Sacrorum Rituum* (5 vols., et 2 appendices, Romae: Ex Typographia Polyglotta, 1898-1927), n. 2767 (hereafter cited *Decr. Auth.*).

omitted, need not be supplied. The same can be said of the clothing of the ordinand with the amice, the maniple and the tunic. The amice is not to be kept over the head during the reading of the prayer, but the bishop is simply to touch the head with the amice and then immediately adjust it around the neck of the ordinand.[75]

B. *The Diaconate*

a) *Defects in Essential Rites*

In the ordination of a deacon, the bishop, after reading the four prayers of introduction according to the instruction of the Pontifical, holds his arms extended before his chest while intoning the words of the preface. Towards the end of this prayer, each of the ordinands approaches the bishop, who imposes his right hand upon the ordinand's head while reciting the prayer "*Accipe Spiritum Sanctum. . . .*" Thereafter the bishop continues with the intonation of the preface, beginning with the words "*Emitte in eos, quaesumus, Domine . . .* ," during which he holds his right hand extended towards the ordinands.[76]

The imposition of the right hand of the bishop upon the head of each ordinand during the recitation of the formula "*Accipe Spiritum Sanctum . . .*" was considered to be the essential matter of the rite of this ordination. The extension of the right hand during the remainder of the preface was looked upon as a moral continuation of the first imposition; the Holy Office, however, held as valid an ordination in which the bishop omitted this extension during the prayer "*Emitte in eos, quaesumus, Domine . . .* ," provided that the first imposition had been accomplished.[77] No mention is made of the need of supplying this part of the rite even privately.

[75] S.R.C., *Veronen.*, 11 sept. 1847, ad 2—*Decr. Auth.*, n. 2956.

[76] *Pontificale Romanum*, Tit. *De Ordinatione Diaconi.*

[77] S.C.S. Off., 7 sept. 1892: "Ordinatio diaconalis valet, etsi Episcopus dexteram nullatenus extenderat versus ordinandos, postquam ea tetigerat caput ordinandi."—A private response found in *Periodica*, XXI (1932), 159; Father Hecht also pointed to two relatively recent replies of the Sacred Congregation of the Sacraments (4 nov. 1912, and 9 mart. 1923) and to one of the Holy Office (27 apr. 1923), giving this same answer.

The bishop was physically to touch the head of the ordinand during the imposition of the right hand, although a physical contact was considered to have taken place when the subject wore a skullcap during the ordination.[78] The replies of the Holy Office at first commanded only the supplying of the physical contact when it was lacking; [79] later responses were clear in commanding that the *whole* ordination be repeated conditionally.[80]

No response was forthcoming with reference to the specific formula of words essential to the rite of ordination to the diaconate. Authors who wrote prior to the constitution *Sacramentum Ordinis* generally held that one of two prayers in the preface of the Mass of ordination specified the imposition of the right hand of the bishop and gave it meaning as the essential rite of this ordination. Conte a Coronata,[81] following Many,[82] held that

78 S.C.S. Off., *Chan-Tong-Me,* 22 ian. 1890—*Collectanea S. Congregationis de Propaganda Fide* (2 vols., Romae: Ex Typographia Polyglotta, S.C. de Propaganda Fide, 1907), n. 1723 (hereafter cited *Collectanea*).

79 S.C.S. Off., *Cocincin.,* 19 aug. 1851: "Iuxta ius canonicum, in Ordinatione presbyteri et diaconi, impositio manuum fieri debet *tactu corporali;* quod si omissum esset, sed dubitatur: 1. Utrum si facta fuerit impositio manuum *tactu corporali,* suppleri debeat impositio manuum tacto corporali? . 3. Si suppleri debeat *tactus corporalis,* an iteranda sint verba quae simul ab Episcopo proferuntur cum impositione manuum, praesertim in Ordinatione diaconi, in qua verba *Accipe Spiritum Sanctum,* etc., *videntur* multis esse forma Sacramenti? R. ad 1 Affirmative. . . ad 3. Affirmative." —*Collectanea,* n. 1066; *Codicis Iuris Canonici Fontes,* cura Emi Card. Gasparri editi (9 vols., Romae: Typis Polyglottis Vaticaniis, 1923-1939; Vols., VII-IX, ed. cura et studio Emi Iustiniani Car. Serédi), n. 917 (hereafter cited *Fontes*).

80 S.C.S. Off., 20 ian. 1875: "Episcopus N. subdiacono diaconatus Ordinem conferre volens, in illius ordinatione peragendo manum utique dexteram, et ad minimam quidem distantiam, super caput eius suspendit, quin tamen praedictum illius caput corporaliter attingeret. 1. An ad reparandum praedictae ordinationis defectum, ordinatio tota diaconatus in illo sacerdote iterari debeat. 2. An haec ordinationis iteratio sub conditione fieri possit a quocumque catholico Episcopo secreto, quocumque anni tempore, etiam in sacello privato. R. Ad utrumque: Affirmative, facto verbo cum SSmo."—*Acta Santae Sedis* (41 vols., Romae, 1865-1908), XXX (1897-1898), 157-158 (hereafter cited *ASS*); *Collectanea,* n. 1431; *Fontes,* n. 1038.

81 *Institutiones Iuris Canonici, De Sacramentis Tractatus Canonicus* (3 vols., Vol. II, *De Ordine,* Torino, 1945), II, n. 221, p. 276.

82 *Praelectiones de Sacra Ordinatione,* n. 268.

this prayer was the *"Emitte in eos, quaesumns, Domine, . . ."* which followed the actual imposition of the hand of the bishop and continued to the end of the preface. They held this opinion because of the antiquity of the prayer and because this formula seemed to be more apt to express the powers conferred in the ordination of a deacon. Gasparri [83] and others [84] preferred to find the essential words of the form in the prayer *"Accipe Spiritum Sanctum . . ."* which accompanies the actual imposition of the hand of the bishop. Gasparri seemed ready to admit that an ordination to the diaconate without this formula would be valid, since such an ordination was valid in the ancient Church before the prayer *"Accipe"* was introduced. But he also held that an ordination in which the preface or eucharistic prayer was omitted and only the prayer *"Accipe"* used would also be valid because, as he argued, although this prayer was not in itself sufficient to determine the imposition of the hand of the bishop as giving powers proper to the deacon, taken in the context of the whole ceremony it was sufficient. Conte a Coronata admits that this opinion has probability, and concludes his opinion with the practical advice that in the administration of this sacrament only a most safe course is to be followed. Thus, if any omissions occur in this ceremony with reference to the prayers mentioned above, the whole ordination should be repeated absolutely or conditionally as the case might demand.[85]

b) *Defects in Integral Rites*

Contrary to the pronouncement of the Council of Florence [86] and the opinion of many of the earlier canonists and theologians, the *Traditio* of the book of the Gospels was not considered essential to this rite of ordination by the Sacred Congregations. Therefore, when this rite was wholly omitted, or when it was not

[83] *De Sacra Ordinatione,* II, 1049.

[84] Alphonsus Liguori, *Theologia Moralia,* Lib. VI, n. 748; Cappello, *De Sacra Ordinatione* (1. ed., Romae, 1935), n. 201.

[85] *De Sacramentis Tractatus Canonicus,* II (1. ed., 1945), n. 221, pp. 276-277.

[86] *Supra,* p. 35.

executed by the bishop personally, or when the book was not touched by one of the ordinands, not the whole ordination was to be repeated, but only the defective rite was to be repaired.[87] This could be done privately, even outside Mass.

c) *Defects in Incidental Rites*

All else, including the investiture with the insignia of the office of deacon—the stole and the dalmatic—constituted only an incidental part of the rite and, when it had been neglected, there was no need for these parts to be supplied.

C. *The Priesthood*

a) *Defects in Essential Rites*

According to the decisions of the Sacred Congregations, the moral union of three rites was considered necessary for the validity of an ordination to the priesthood: The first imposition of hands by the bishop in silence,[88] the second imposition or extension of the right hand of the bishop over the head of the ordinand during the prayer "*Oremus, fratres carissimi . . . ,*"[89] and the delivery, by the bishop, of the chalice with wine and the paten with the host together with the words "*Accipe potestatem offerre sacrificium Deo. . . .*"[90]

At the first imposition of hands the bishop must physically

[87] S.R.C., *Taurinen.*, 16 iun. 1837: "Ordinatio diaconorum, in qua porrectus non est liber evangeliorum, minime iteranda est, sed Episcopus suppleat traditionem istius libri proferendo verba "Accipe potestatem legendi evangelium. . . ."—*Dect. Auth.*, n. 2767.

[88] "Pontifex stans ante faldistorium suum cum mitra, et nulla oratione, nulloque cantu praemissis, imponit simul utramque manum super caput cuiuslibet ordinandi successive nihil dicens."—*Pontificale Romanum,* Tit. *De Ordinatione Presbyteri.*

[89] "Quo facto, tam Pontifex, quam Sacerdotes, tenent manus dexteras extensas super illos. Et Pontifex stans cum mitra dicit . . ."—*Loc. cit.*

[90] Before the revision of the rubrics of the Pontifical by the Congregation of Sacred Rites (*AAS,* XLII (1950), 448-455) the general rubrics concerning the conferring of Orders cautioned the bishop thus: "Moneat ordinandos, quod instrumenta, in quorum traditione character imprimitur, tangant . . ."—*Ibid.,* Tit. *De Ordinibus Conferendis.*

touch the head of the ordinand.[91] Since the bishop is wearing gloves during the rite, it matters not whether the head of the ordinand is covered or not.[92]

With reference to the second imposition of the hands of the bishop, this must take place in union with the prayer "*Oremus, fratres carissimi. . . .*" The Holy Office had judged that the two are sufficiently united when the bishop holds his right hand extended only after or towards the end of the prayer,[93] or before the beginning of the prayer, though not while it is being said,[94] or during the prayer only, but not for the time between the first and the second imposition of hands.[95]

If one or both of the first two impositions are substantially defective and this is noticed before the *traditio instrumentorum,* the defect may be supplied within the ceremony at that point. In this case the ordination is certainly valid.[96] If the supply is made, however, only after the delivery of the chalice and the paten, the whole ordination is to be repeated conditionally.[97]

In the third essential rite, the delivery of the chalice and the paten, both instruments must be personally handed to the ordinands by the bishop and physically touched by them. Since this rite follows the anointing of hands in the ceremony, the hands of the ordinands are, at the time when the chalice and the paten are presented, bound with a linen cloth. The rubrics give the following directions for the touching of the chalice and the paten:

[91] S.C.S. Off:. *Cocincin.,* 19 aug. 1851—*Collectanea,* n. 1066; *Fontes,* n. 917. Also, S.C.S. Off., 4 iul. 1900—*Fontes,* n. 1241.

[92] Cf. S.C.S. Off., *Chan-Tong-Me,* 22 ian. 1890—*Collectanea,* n. 1723.

[93] S.C.S. Off., 12 sept. 1877—*Collectanea,* n. 1482.

[94] S.R.C., *Syren.,* 14 iun. 1873—*Decr. Auth.,* n. 3307.

[95] *Loc. cit.* The Holy Office (19 iul. 1899) commanded that the ordination be repeated conditionally when a bishop, after the first imposition of hands, extended his arms only to hold the book during the prayers that followed. The slight extension of the arms that was required to hold the book was not judged sufficient to positively fulfill the requirements for validity in this case. Cf. *Fontes,* n. 1226.

[96] S.C.S. Off., 3 maii 1899—*Collectanea,* n. 2047.

[97] S.C.S. Off., 22 aug. 1900—*Collectanea,* n. 2292.

> Tum tradit cuilibet successive Calicem cum vino, et aqua, et Patenam superpositum cum hostia, et ipsi illam accipiunt inter indices et medios digitos, et cuppam calicis et patenam simul tangunt . . . [98]

The Sacred Congregation held that, as in the ordination of a subdeacon, the chalice and the paten were to be considered as one unit. Thus, when the ordinand touched the chalice and the host, but not the paten,[99] or if he touched only the paten and the host, but not the chalice,[100] or if he touched only the chalice,[101] the ordination was valid.

This was also true when the ordinand touched the vessels with his thumb and index finger, rather than with his index and middle fingers, or when the ordinand first touched the instruments, but afterwards, while the bishop was pronouncing the form, lost contact with the vessels.[102] According to the rubrics the chalice must contain wine mixed with a small amount of water. It was held sufficient for validity if the chalice contained matter substantially adequate for consecration. Thus, wine alone proved sufficient, and so did any mixture in which there was more wine than water in all probability.[103] On the other hand, the ordination was to be repeated conditionally if the chalice was empty,[104] or contained water only,[105] or contained as much or more water than wine.[106] This defect could be repaired within the ceremony, if done immediately. However, if the rite was supplied only after the communion or even before the third imposition of hands, no repair was effected. In these cases the entire ordination was to be repeated conditionally.

[98] *Pontificale Romanum,* Tit. *De Ordinatione Presbyteri.*

[99] S.C.S. Off., 2 iul. 1892—*Collectanea,* n. 1900.

[100] S.C.S. Off., 17 mart. 1897—*Collectanea,* n. 1963.

[101] S.C.S. Off., 7 sept. 1897—*ASS,* XXX (1897-1898), 286.

[102] S.C.S. Off., 17 mart. 1897—*ASS,* XXIX (1896-1897), 703-704.

[103] S.C.S. Off., 11 apr. 1932—A private response reported by Vermeersch in *Periodica,* XXII (1933), 134.

[104] S.C.S. Off., 11 ian. 1899—*Collectanea,* n. 2032; *Fontes,* n. 1213.

[105] S.C.S. Off., 17 mart. 1897—*Collectanea,* n. 1963; *Fontes,* n. 1160.

[106] S.C.S. Off., *Angliae,* 7 sept. 1892—*Collectanea,* n. 1811.

Here again, as in the ordination of a deacon, no definite response can be cited as a guide in the determination of the formula of words essential in the ordination of a priest. It can be said, however, that the few responses given above did somewhat narrow the limits of the historic controversy.[107] Of the many opinions put forward in the course of time only those which held to the essential nature of the imposition of hands accomplished in silence and continued through the preface and the *traditio* of the chalice and paten were supported by the responses of the Sacred Congregations. Speculative opinion prior to the year 1948 centered upon the words of the preface as the essential formula of words necessary for the validity of this ordination.[108] The invitatory *"Oremus, fratres carissimi . . ."* and the prayer *"Exaudi nos, quaesumus, . . ."* were generally considered only introductory to and not a part of this essential formula.[109] As a practical precaution against invalidity the whole ordination was to be repeated conditionally if the prayer *"Accipe potestatem . . ."* accompanying the *Traditio instrumentorum* was omitted or substantially corrupted.[110]

b) *Defects in Integral Rites*

Two rites were considered necessary for the integrity, but not for the validity, of the ordination. These were the anointing of the hands of the ordinands and the third or last imposition of the hands by the bishop, which took place after the communion of the Mass. If the whole rite of anointing had been omitted, it was to be supplied with the use of the words of the formulary given in the Pontifical. When the oil of chrism or the oil of the sick was used instead of the oil of catechumens, as prescribed by the Pontifical, the rite was not considered defective, and nothing was to be supplied.[111] Likewise, if the bishop pronounced only

[107] *Supra*, pp. 33-42.

[108] Cf. Gasparri, *De Sacra Ordinatione*, n. 1079.

[109] Many, *Praelectiones de Sacra Ordinatione*, n. 259; *contra* Cappello, *De Sacra Ordinatione* (1. ed., 1935), n. 218.

[110] Cappello, *De Sacra Ordinatione*, n. 218, § 7.

[111] S.C.S. Off., 22 iul. 1874—*Collectanea*, n. 1421.

part of the prayer to be said during the anointing, but completed the form with the intention of including all the ordinands when he anointed the hands of the last candidate, the prior anointings were not to be repeated.[112]

The last imposition of hands was held to be defective and in need of repair when a bishop failed to use the prescribed form "*Accipe Spiritum Sanctum* . . . ," or when he failed to touch physically the head of the candidate.[113] In repairing the rite the bishop was to repeat only the imposition of hands and the prayer, and not the incidental rites closely connected with this action in the ordination ceremony, such as the unfolding of the chasuble or the acceptance of the obedience.[114]

c) *Defects in Incidental Rites*

If, according to the custom of the place, the imposition of hands was omitted by all or a part of the priests present, there was no need for any supplying of this ceremony.[115] The clothing with the stole and the chasuble, the recitation of the Mass together with the bishop, as also the promise of obedience were considered incidental rites and thus were not so important to the ordination as signs of the powers conferred that they called for a supplying of these rites at a later time in the event they had been omitted. Gasparri, however, recommended that the promise of obedience be supplied, not because of its importance to the ceremony, but because of its significance as a token of submission to the bishop.[116]

D. *The Episcopate*

a) *Defects in Essential Rites*

The responses of the Sacred Congregations gave no direct indication of the necessary rite in episcopal consecration. The common opinion of later canonists and theologians, however, provided a safe norm for action and practice. The essential rite

[112] S.C.S. Off., 28 nov. 1900—*ASS,* XXXIII (1900-1901), 374-375.

[113] S.C.S. Off., 27 maii 1840—*Fontes,* n. 880.

[114] S.C.S. Off., 9 dec. 1897—*Collectanea,* n. 1978.

[115] S.C. de Prop. Fide., *Pro Sin.,* 6 aug. 1840—*Collectanea,* n. 908.

[116] *De Sacra Ordinatione,* n. 1020.

in an episcopal consecration was generally held to be the imposition of hands by the bishop consecrator and the two assisting bishops, who with physical contact touched the head of the bishop elect during the prayer "*Accipe Spiritum Sanctum,*" together with the extension of hands made by all three while the consecrator intoned the words of the preface.[117] Of all the words of the preface, Many considered the following the more important and as sufficing for an expression of the essential form of this Order:

> *Et idcirco huic famulo tuo, quem ad summi sacerdotii ministerium elegisti, hanc quaesumus, Domine, gratiam largiaris; ut quidquid illa velamina in fulgore auri, in nitore gremmarum, et in multimodi operis varietate signabant, hoc in eius moribus actibusque clarescat. Comple in sacerdote tuo ministerii tui summam et ornamentis totius glorificationis instructum coelestis unguenti rore sanctifica. Hoc, Domine, copiose in caput eius influat; hoc in oris subiecta decurrat; hoc in totius corporis extrema descendat: ut tui Spiritus virtus et interiora eius repleat, et exteriora circumtegat. Abundet in eo constantia fidei, puritas dilectionis, sinceritas pacis.*" [118]

The words, *Accipe Spiritum Sanctum,*" were not generally considered essential to this rite after the pronouncement of Pope Leo XIII concerning Anglican Orders. In the Apostolic Letter *Apostolicae curae,* issued on September 13, 1896, the Roman Pontiff declared this formula alone was not sufficient to express the office and power of episcopal Orders.[119] When the assisting bishops omitted this rite, caution dictated that the whole rite be repeated conditionally, for it was not known whether the consecrator acted singly or in union with the two assisting bishops.[120] Pope Pius XII, in the Apostolic Constitution dated November 30, 1944, clarified this point in declaring that the validity of

[117] Wernz-Vidal, *Ius Canonicum* (7 vols. in 9, Romae: Apud Aedes Universitatis Gregorianae, 1923-1938), Vol. IV, *De Rebus,* Pars 1, n. 268.

[118] *Praelectiones de Sacra Ordinatione,* n. 193.

[119] § 9: "De consecratione episcopali similiter est. Nam formulae, *Accipe Spiritum Sanctum,* non modo serius adnexa sunt verba, *ad officium et opus episcopi,* sed etiam de iisdem . . . iudicandum aliter est quam in ritu Catholico."—*Fontes,* n. 631.

[120] Gasparri, *op. cit.,* n. 1088.

an episcopal consecration demanded only one bishop consecrator. He stated further that the two assisting bishops were demanded for the lawfulness of the consecration, and were to be called, thenceforth, not assisting bishops, but co-consecrators. To fulfill their office they must, like the consecrator, touch the head of the bishop-elect with both hands while saying the prayer "*Accipe Spiritum Sanctum*," and also recite all the prayers together with the consecrator, although in a low tone. They must also have, like the consecrator, the intention of consecrating.[121] More will be said about the office of the co-consecrator in a later chapter.[122]

b) *Defects in Integral Rites*

Three rites were considered integral to the consecration of a bishop: The *traditio* of the book of the gospels, the anointing of the hands and the head of the bishop-elect with chrism, and the profession of faith. The rubrics give the following direction for the delivery of the book:

> *Tum Consecrator accipit librum Evangeliorum de scapulis Consecrati; et adiuvantibus ipsum Episcopis assistentibus, tradit eum clausum Consecrato, tangenti illum sine apertione manuum dicens: . . .*[123]

If the handing over of the book of the gospels with the accompanying words was omitted, that rite alone was to be supplied. This was not so certain when the book was not placed upon the head and shoulders of the candidate. It was thought by many that this rite should also be supplied in view of its antiquity.[124]

If the rite of anointing the head and the hands of the candidate with chrism had been omitted, it had to be supplied according to the instructions of Pope Innocent III, as noted above.[125] This was to be done by three bishops, who were to use the formula found in the Pontifical. The words of the Council of Trent

121 *AAS,* XXXVII (1945), 131-132.

122 *Infra,* p. 76.

123 *Pontificale Romanum,* Tit. *De Consecratione Electi in Episcopum.*

124 Many, *op. cit.,* n. 297, § 2.

125 *Supra,* p. 28.

were also quoted in support of this action. The fifth canon treating of the sacrament of Orders stated:

> *Si quis dixerit sacram unctionem, qua Ecclesia in sancto ordinatione utitur, non tantum non requiri, sed contemnendam et perniciosam esse, similiter et alias ordinis caeremonias, anathema sit.*[126]

The profession of the faith to be made by the bishop-elect before the consecration is not properly a part of the rite of an episcopal consecration, if, however, for any reason it was omitted, the profession was to be supplied at a later time.[127]

c) *Defects in Incidental Rites*

The other rites of episcopal consecration may in no way be neglected, but when they have been omitted or have not been properly or completely performed no repair of the rite is necessary. These rites include the handing over of the ring, of the miter, or of the crozier. When the examination before the consecration has been omitted, recourse should be had to the Holy See.[128]

Article IV. The Law Prior to the Constitution

The foregoing pages have shown that long before the promulgation of the Code of Canon Law a uniform practice had developed in the Church regarding the repair of defective rites in the ordination ceremony. This practice was divided into two general modes of procedure: That which treated of the repair of essential defects, which touch the validity of the Order received, and that which treated the repair of defects which in no way affected the validity of the Order, but were gravely offensive to the integrity of the rites through which the Order was conferred. In the first case the Church demanded the repetition of the entire rite of ordination either absolutely or conditionally; in the second a supplying of the rites was ordered if they had proved deficient.

[126] Sessio XXIII, *De sacramento ordinis,* can. 5—Schroeder, *Canons and Decrees of the Council of Trent,* pp. 163, 435.

[127] S.C. Prop. Fide, 10 ian. 1875—*Collectanea,* n. 1429.

[128] Cappello, *De Sacra Ordinatione,* n. 241, § 9.

The introduction of the Code of Canon Law made no change in this practice as it had developed. While one such canon was proposed, the redactors of the Code chose not to treat this matter directly. They did, however, provide a supplementary norm, which in the absence of specific legislation established the directive for the repair of defective rites. This was the *praxis curiae,* of which mention was made in canon 20. Many of the decrees of the Congregations mentioned above have an obligatory force all their own by reason of the fact that they can be proved to be a *Decretum Generale,* or, by reason of their content, equivalently general; others are and remain particular decrees, binding only those to whom they were addressed. Reference is made here, however, not to the particular legal force of the individual decrees but to the overall *praxis* which has been outlined in the preceding article. The officially issued responses, not only in their style or form, but also in the matter which they contain, when a repeated application had been made in the same way over a period of time, grew into the estate of law. The consistent approach of the Roman Congregations to the problem of defective rites in sacred ordinations as characterized by the two principles mentioned above shows forth the *stylus curiae;* the classification of those ceremonies which are of the substance and integrity of the rites has been the result of the practice of the Roman Curia. Both bind the minister of ordination to the repair of defective rites, and specify how this obligation is to be fulfilled; only the latter was to become partially amended by the Apostolic Constitution *Sacramentum Ordinis.*

CHAPTER 4

THE REPAIR OF DEFECTIVE RITES IN THE PRESENT LAW

ARTICLE I. THE APOSTOLIC CONSTITUTION *Sacramentum Ordinis*

On November 30, 1947, all doubt concerning the matter and the form of the sacrament of Orders which had commanded the attention of theologians in endless debate since the thirteenth century, and which had dictated the caution policies of the Sacred Congregations in repairing the rites of sacred ordination, was definitely dispelled. At that time Pope Pius XII, in the Apostolic Constitution *Sacramentum Ordinis,* decreed that at least for the future the *traditio instrumentorum* was not the essential matter of the sacrament of Orders; that the essential matter and form of the Diaconate, of the Priesthood, and of the Episcopate were to be found in the first and principal imposition of hands accompanied with the words of the preface of the ceremony which determine this action; that the imposition of hands required for the validity of the sacrament did not need to be effected or executed by means of a physical contact, inasmuch as a moral imposition of hands was sufficient.[1]

The history of the difficulties resolved by this authoritative pronouncement has been delineated in the foregoing chapters. For the present all doubt is removed as to the exact moment when the candidate receives the grace and the power of the Order to which he is being ordained. The task remains of applying this new information to the specification of the duties of the minister of major Orders with reference to the supplying of rites that have proved defective. The writer proposes to examine the Constitution in some detail with a view to determining the exact inten-

[1] *AAS,* XL (1948), 5-6; for the convenience of the reader the Latin text and an English translation of the Constitution have been printed in an appendix to this work. Henceforth reference will be made to this appendix. *Infra,* pp. 100-105.

tion of the Holy Father and the particular character of his pronouncement.

A. *The Purpose and Nature of the Constitution*

The Constitution begins with a recital of several dogmatic facts fundamental to sacramental theology. The sacrament of Orders, instituted by Christ, is one and the same for the universal Church. Of the seven sacraments entrusted to the Church by Christ, the Church has never substituted another; nor can it do so, for, according to the Council of Trent, the Church has no power over the *substance of the sacraments*.[2] Finally, the term *substance of the sacraments* is defined as "those things which, as the source of divine revelation bears witness, Christ Himself set up for observance in the sacramental sign."[3]

The second paragraph of the Constitution reveals the purpose of the Supreme Pontiff in issuing the decree. Although the unity and identity of the sacrament had never been denied, so he states, the addition of various rites in the course of time gave rise to theological controversy concerning the matter and the form of the sacrament. This in turn has been a cause of doubts and anxieties in particular cases concerning the validity of the Orders received. As if to emphasize his twofold purpose—the end of controversy and the preclusion of doubts of conscience—the Pontiff repeats his reasons immediately before his solemn declaration or decree concerning the matter and the form of the sacrament of Orders.[4]

The theological controversy is the first to be resolved. Here the problem is centered in the *Decretum pro Armenis*. Was a change effected in the matter and the form of the sacrament? If

[2] The full decree of the Council in Session XXI, Chapter 2, reads: "Praeterea declarat, hanc potestatem perpetuo in ecclesia fuisse, ut in sacramentorum dispensatione, salva illorum substantia, ea statueret vel mutaret, quae suscipientium utilitati seu ipsorum sacramentorum venerationi pro rerum, temporum et locorum varietate magis expedire judicaret." —Schroeder, *Canons and Decrees of the Council of Trent*, p. 407.

[3] ". . . ea quae, testibus divinae revelationis fontibus, ipse Christus Dominus in signo sacramentali servanda statuit."

[4] "Hinc consequitur ut declaremus, sicut revera ad omnem controversiam auferendam et ad conscientiarum anxietatibus viam percludendam, . . ."

it is said that the matter and the form of the sacrament were changed, then it follows that the Church has the power to bring about such a change, since it is admitted by all that the *traditio instrumentorum* was not known in the early days of the Church. An affirmation of this kind would vindicate the opinion of those who attribute this power to the Church in asserting the generic, albeit immediate, institution of the sacrament of Orders by Christ.

On the other hand, if it is said that no change was effected by the decree of the Council of Florence, this would give strength to the argument of those who hold that the Church does not have such power. These hold that the matter and the form of the sacrament and its substance are identifiable concepts, and thus the Church has no power to change or alter that which was specifically instituted by Christ as the sensible sign of the sacrament of Orders. In order to put an end to controversy without choosing between these two legitimate schools of thought, the Holy Father uses a conditional form of argumentation, first proposed by Cardinal Gasparri in presenting this very problem to the Sacred Congregation of the Sacraments before the promulgation of the Code of Canon Law.[5]

Inasmuch as the Fathers of the Council of Florence did not require the *traditio instrumentorum* for a valid ordination in the Greek Church when it was received back into union at that Council, so the Holy Father argues, it cannot be said that this requirement was made of the Armenian Church for the essence and the validity of the sacrament in fulfillment of the will of Christ, or, in other words, because it constituted a part of the substance of the sacrament. Therefore, if the *traditio instrumentorum* was required of the Armenians, this requirement proceeded from the *will of the Church,* and was exercised in an area within which the Church was competent to make such demands. But what the Church establishes, She can also abrogate. Therefore, if the tradition of the instruments was ever required for the validity of sacred Orders, this requirement is now abrogated, and, for the future at least, is not required for the validity of the sacrament from the will and the prescription of the Church.

[5] Hürth, "Commentarium ad Constitutionem Apostolicam," *Periodica,* XXXVII (1948), 10; *supra,* p. 23.

Having disposed of the controversy, the Supreme Pontiff proceeds to a positive affirmation of the sensible signs of the sacrament of Orders. But even here he offers no comfort to either school of thought concerning the manner in which Christ instituted the sacraments. In order to allow for the two possibilities mentioned above, he employs two terms in juxtaposition throughout the Constitution.[6]

Calling upon his Supreme Apostolic Authority, the Pontiff declares (*declaramus*) and decrees (*decernimus, disponimus, statuimus*) the essential matter and form of the sacrament of Orders. The declaration (an indication of that which was always true independently of the declaration) is followed by and opposed to his positive disposition regarding the same subject (an indication of what will be the rule from the moment of its implementation) which is made only conditionally (*quatenus opus sit; si umquam aliter legitime dispositum fuerit*). If what is now to be established as the matter and the form of the sacrament was not always so, then he disposes that it be so for the future.[7] That is, that

> The one and sole matter of the Sacred Orders of the Diaconate, of the Priesthood and of the Episcopate is the imposition of hands, and likewise that the one and only form consists in the words which determine the application of this matter by which are univocally signified the sacramental effects which as such—namely the power of Orders and the grace of the Holy Spirit—are accepted and employed by the Church.[8]

[6] Cardinal Gasparri, in proposing to the Congregation of the Holy Office the solution to the problem of the matter and the form of the sacrament of Orders, remarked that all must accept the conclusion of his argument, though with this possible difference: some would say that such a decree only *declared* that to be which always was, while others would claim that the decree *restored* the question to the state in which it was before (Hürth, "art. cit.," p. 10). The Holy Father makes every allowance for the two points of view.

[7] Cf. Crosignani, "Annotationes ad Constitutionem Apostolicam de Sacris Ordinibus Diaconatus, Presbyteratus et Episcopatus," *Divus Thomas: Commentarium de Philosophia et Theologia* (Piacenza: Series Tertia, 1924-), XXV (1948), 162.

[8] *Infra*, p. 102.

In the sixth paragraph of the Constitution the Holy Father proceeds to specify in exact detail the imposition of hands and the precise formula of words used to signify the sacramental effects in each of the Orders. These words will be examined in a later article. Let it be sufficient to say here that this paragraph serves well the second purpose of the Constitution—the preclusion of doubts of conscience concerning the validity of an ordination conferred. Because there could be some doubt as to when the provisions of this Constitution take effect, further avenues of doubt are forestalled when the Supreme Pontiff in the concluding paragraph of the Constitution determines that "the provisions of this Our Constitution do not have retroactive force." [9]

The purpose of this valuable and important papal pronouncement has been adequately explored for the purposes at hand. What of the nature of the Constitution? The Most Reverend Francisco Miranda Vicente, Auxiliary Bishop of Toledo, in an address to the First International Congress of Pastoral Liturgy held in Assisi, Italy, expressed very well the dual nature of the Constitution when he stated:

> This Apostolic Constitution is a true and solemn dogmatic declaration, and at the same time, as the terms used in the fourth and fifth points indicate, it is a doctrinal and disciplinary decree.[10]

The doctrinal nature of this papal document cannot or should not be minimized. To quote but one instance, the term "substance of the sacrament" is for the first time officially defined in this Constitution. In addition to the many direct statements as to the nature and operation of the sacrament of Orders, many indirect arguments can be found in its pages for the enrichment of sacramental theology. Viewing the Constitution in the light of the express purpose the Holy Father had in its promulgation, however, the more precise nature of the Constitution must be found in its dispositive and disciplinary parts, wherein are found the bulk of its provisions and the height of its import. The doctrinal must certainly be distinguished from the disciplinary as-

[9] "Huius Nostrae Constitutionis dispositiones vim retroactivam non habent; . . ."

[10] *The Assisi Papers* (Collegeville, Minn.: Liturgical Press, 1957), p. 136.

pects of the Constitution, for the former are most definitely retroactive. The major part of the Constitution, however, is nonretroactive, and this point alone establishes these provisions as points of positive ecclesiastical law.[11]

It can be concluded, then, that the nature of this Constitution is essentially dispositive and disciplinary. Although doctrinal truths are incorporated in the text, and even though the disciplinary measures found therein have doctrinal overtones, the primary dispositions have the character of laws, and accordingly are to be judged and applied according to legal principles.[12]

Do these disciplinary provisions have binding force at the very moment of promulgation or only after a lapse of time? The Constitution has nothing to say concerning this matter. There-

[11] Cf. Mors, *Theologia Fundamentalis* (2 vols., Bonis Auris, Argentina: Typis "Editorial Guadalupe," 1954), II, 139.

[12] In treating of the sacraments one cannot always clearly draw the fine line between doctrinal and disciplinary decrees. Canon George Smith (1893-1960) the well-known English theologian, remarked: "Let us then clearly distinguish two powers of the Church: her supreme power of teaching revealed truth and her supreme power of administering the sacraments. . . . This (the latter) is the authority to which the Fathers of the Council of Trent appealed as enabling the Church 'to make such dispositions and changes in the dispensation of the sacraments—always saving their substance—as she may judge expedient [Sess. XXI, cap. 2].' It is not an infallible authority to teach revealed truth, it is a divinely constituted power—equally committed to her by Christ—of so regulating the administration of the sacraments that they may remain surely and unfailingly the sacred rites which were instituted by her divine Founder.

"But if this administrative power of the Church is distinct from her infallible *magisterium* it is by no means divorced from it. The subject matter of each frequently coincides, for the Church can and often does make doctrinal pronouncements concerning the sacraments. . . . But the two powers are more closely connected still. When the Church uses her Christ-given authority to make regulations or changes in regard to the sacred rites, although her action is directly administrative and not didactic, it carries with it a doctrinal implication. For it is implicit in such regulations and dispositions that they are made within the framework which Christ immutably shaped, and that the sacrament so regulated and administered is authentically and 'substantially' the rite which He instituted. And because this is a matter in which the Church cannot err, such regulations are rightly said to fall within the scope of indirect infallibility." —"The Church and Her Sacraments," *The Clergy Review* (London, 1931-), XXXIII (1950), 224-226.

fore, the principle as it is stated in canon 9 must be employed. Since a greater or lesser lapse of time was not designated, the law began to have binding force after a lapse of three months from the date on which the Constitution was promulgated in the *Acta Apostolicae Sedis*—January 28, 1948. Thus the law acquired full force from midnight between the 27th and 28th of April, 1948. All ordinations which took place on or after the 28th of April of that year are to be judged by the principles of the Constitution; all ordinations which took place before this date must be judged according to the law then flourishing and reflected in the practice of the Roman Congregations.[13]

Considered as a purely disciplinary decree, the provisions of the Constitution *Sacramentum Ordinis* extend only to subjects of the Latin Rite. Actually, except for the Armenian Church, the problems solved by the Constitution existed only in the West, for the Churches of the Oriental Rite did not nor do they now employ the *traditio instrumentorum* in the ceremony of ordination. An analogous application of canon 1, however, would bind these Churches with regard to the doctrinal implications contained in the Constitution.[14] The imposition of hands, for instance, must be universally recognized as a sufficient sign of the transfer of power and grace in the ordination ceremony, when specified by words which are suited for giving expression to this transfer and are so employed by the Church. On the other hand, the Churches of the East would not be bound by the exact form of words mentioned in the Constitution as essential to each of the Orders. At least one writer is of the opinion that the pronouncement of the Holy Father would have force in the Oriental Churches in this sense, that anyone ordained according to the Constitution would be validly ordained.[15] This statement is most probably true. But what of the possibility that, at some time in the history of the Church, some requirement was made of one of the Oriental Rites that it add some specific ritual action to its cere-

[13] Damen, "In Constitutionem Apostolicam *Sacramentum Ordinis* a Pio XII Latam d. 28 ian. 1948: Analysis et Commentarium," *Euntes Docete* (Romae: 1948-), I (1948), 111.

[14] Smith, "art. cit.," *The Clergy Review,* XXVIII (1950), p. 226, fn. 1.

[15] Damen, "art. cit.," *Euntes Docete,* I (1948), 108.

mony of ordination? And let it be posited further that this action was required for the validity of the ordination from "the will of the Church." This is exactly what some authors claim was effected by the *Decretum pro Armenis* for the Armenian Church. If the *traditio instrumentorum* was required for the validity of ordinations in the Armenian Church (many affirm that it was not), it must be said that it was only required from "the will of the Church." The Holy Father has established that what the Church can demand, She can also take away. But, is this requirement, if it was made, taken away by the wording of the Constitution *Sacramentum Ordinis?* From the nature of the Constitution and, inasmuch as no specific mention is made of the Oriental Church, it must be concluded that it was not taken away. Thus, if, for example, the *traditio instrumentorum* were to be omitted in an ordination performed in the Armenian Liturgy, it would seem that such an ordination would be doubtful and the doubt would have to be referred to the Holy See for a solution.

B. *Cases of Doubt*

The Constitution provides that any cases of doubt regarding the application of the various points contained in the decree are to be submitted to the Apostolic See for judgment.[16] This involves no change in the customary practice of the Holy See, for the resolving of cases of doubtful ordination is under the exclusive competence of the Congregation of the Sacraments.[17] But, inasmuch as it was the primary purpose of the Constitution to preclude the probability of doubts and scrpules in this area, it stands to reason that cases of doubt will occur with much less frequency now that the matter and the form of the sacrament are no longer a question of dispute.

In view of the clarity of the Constitution, only two possibilities remain for the emergence of doubts concerning the validity of Orders with reference to the essential elements of the sacrament. The first of these obtains when it is doubted whether or

[16] ". . . quod si dubium aliquod contingat, illud huic Apostolicae Sedi erit subiiciendum."—*AAS*, XL (1948), 7.

[17] Canon 249, § 3.

not the imposition of hands took place, or whether at the imposition of hands the minimum requisite moral contact was had. The second of these obtains in all those cases in which it is doubted whether a change in the wording of the form rendered the ordination questionable. In all other cases the ordination is manifestly valid or invalid. Accordingly there should be very few *dubia* presented to the Holy See concerning ordinations which took place or still will take place after April 27, 1948. When the ordination is certainly invalid, the past practice continues to indicate that the whole ordination should be repeated.[18]

What need is there of the supplying of the non-essential rites accidentally omitted in the ordination? Does the Constitution make a change in the developed practice of repairing defects in the rites which contribute to the integrity of the ordination ceremony? Some authors are of the opinion that, inasmuch as no mention of the supplying of non-essential rites is made in the Constitution, recourse must be had to the Holy See in each instance.[19] This opinion, however, seems to unduly extend the terms and purpose of the Constitution. It cannot be reasonably presumed that, in commanding that all doubts concerning the matter and the form of the sacrament of Orders should be presented to the Holy See, the Holy Father wished to overthrow all the established practice of the past with reference to the supplying of non-essential rites that had in some manner proved defective. It was not the specific intention of the Supreme Pontiff to establish new norms for licit conduct in reference to the ceremony of ordination; he simply intended, for the future, to preclude doubts of conscience concerning the validity of the Orders conferred and received. Other secondary disciplinary norms, inasmuch as they do not receive specification, are presumed to retain their force.[20]

[18] *Supra*, p. 54.

[19] Hürth, "Commentarium ad Constitutionem Apostolicam," *Periodica*, XXXVII (1948), 37; Pujolras, "Annotationes," *Commentarium pro Religiosis et Missionariis* [C.p.R.M.] (*Commentarius pro Religiosis* 1920-1934; Romae: 1935-), XXIX (1948), 10; *contra*, Montague, "The Apostolic Constitution on Sacred Orders," *The Irish Ecclesiastical Record* (Dublin: 1864-), 5. Series, LXX (1948), 445.

[20] Canon 23.

C. *The Revision of the Rubrics of the Roman Pontifical*

In order to bring the rubrics of the Roman Pontifical into conformity with the provisions of the Constitution *Sacramentum Ordinis* as well as the earlier Apostolic Constitution *Episcopalis Consecrationis,* the Sacred Congregation of Rites on February 20, 1950, issued a decree amending and correcting the rubrics of the Roman Pontifical and declaring that future editions of the Pontifical should have inserted in its pages the *Variationes in Rubricis Pontificalis Romani* that followed the decree.[21] The full text of the decree as well as the changes it effects in the rubrics of the Roman Pontifical have been included in this work for the convenience of the reader. The complete text forms appendix III of this work.[22] Any future reference to the revised rubrics of the Roman Pontifical will be made with a designation of the page or pages of this appendix.

The first change in the rubrics of the Pontifical is made in the general rubric given under the title *De Ordinibus Conferendis.* Here the instruction that indicated that the character was imprinted with the *traditio instrumentorum* is deleted.[23] In all three sacramental Orders the words of the form are set off in bold and upper case type and the rubics are changed to indicate positively that these are the words of the sacramental form. In order to minimize the possibility of mistakes, the actual words of the form are to be spoken and not chanted.[24] Other changes in the rubrics will be noted in the following article.

Article II. The Orders Considered Individually

A. *The Subdiaconate*

The subdiaconate, the first of the major or sacred Orders, is not mentioned in the Apostolic Constitution. The repair of defective rites with reference to this Order, therefore, continues to be regulated by the practice which obtained before 1948. While the Apostolic Constitution remains without any direct effect upon

[21] *AAS,* XLII (1950), 448-455.

[22] *Infra,* p. 106.

[23] *Infra,* p. 106.

[24] *Infra,* p. 107.

the subdiaconate, it does indirectly confirm the common opinion of theologians [25] which classifies this Order with the minor Orders as institutions founded by the Church in contraposition to the sacramental Orders founded by Christ.[26] Certainly, the distinction between those Orders which employ the *traditio instrumentorum* and those which use the imposition of hands as the essential rite is heightened by the terms of the Constitution.

B. *The Diaconate*

The Apostolic Constitution establishes that in the Order of the diaconate the matter of the sacrament consists in the one imposition of the right hand of the bishop which takes place in that ordination. The form consists in the words of the preface, of which the following are essential and necessary for validity: *Emitte in eum, quaesumus, Domine, Spiritum Sanctum, quo in opus ministerii tui fideliter exsequendi septiformis gratiae tuae munere roboretur.*[27]

In viewing the one imposition of the right hand of the bishop, one must consider neither the position of the bishop's hand during the first part of the preface,[28] nor the extension of the right hand made during the recitation of the essential words of the form,[29] as part of the essential matter of the sacrament. With regard to this last point, the revised rubrics of the Roman Pontifical just referred to are not as clear and unequivocal as the words of the Constitution. Following the recitation of the essential words of the form, the rubrics prescribe that the bishop is to continue to hold his right hand extended until the end of the preface. Parenthetic reference is made to the fact that this last

[25] Cf. Lennerz, *De Sacramento Ordinis,* pp. 114-125.

[26] Crosignani, "art. cit.," *Divus Thomas,* Series III, XXV (1948), 159.

[27] "In Ordinatione Diaconali materia est Episcopi manus impositio quae in ritu istius Ordinationis una occurit. Forma autem constat verbis 'Praefationis' quorum haec sunt essentialia ideoque ad valorem requisita: . . ." —*AAS,* XL (1948), 6.

[28] "Deinde, deposita mitra, extensis manibus ante pectus, dicit . . ."—*Pontificale Romanum, De Ordinatione Diaconi.*

[29] "Postea, extensam tenens manum dexteram, dicit verba formae sacramentalis . . ."—*Infra,* p. 107.

mentioned action is not required for the validity of the ordination.[30] It could be inferred that, since express mention is made of the fact that this continued extension of the hand until the end of the preface is not required for validity, the extension of the bishop's hand during the reading of the words of the form *is* so required.

Father Hecht considered this problem in the pages of *Periodica.*[31] First of all he pointed to several replies of the Congregation of the Sacraments which show that this extension of the right hand of the bishop was not required for the validity of the ordination in the former discipline. The Apostolic Constitution does not contravene this, he stated, for it clearly states that the essential matter of this Order is the one imposition of the hand which takes place in the ordination. Since any judgment is to be made from the wording of the Constitution, and not the rubrics of the Congregation of Sacred Rites, he concluded that the omission of the extension of the right hand of the bishop during the recitation of the essential words of the form in no way affects the validity of the ordination.[32] The action commanded by this rubric must be merely symbolic of what has gone before, and in no way forms a bridge for a necessary moral union of the matter and form of this sacramental ordination.[33]

For the lawful administration of the sacrament the bishop must always physically touch the head of the ordinand during the imposition of the hand.[34] Inasmuch as the bishop is wearing gloves during this part of the ceremony, the notion of physical contact is not compromised by the fact that the ordinand is wearing a skullcap or toupee.[35] When this physical contact is not had, however, a moral contact (*tactus moralis*) suffices for

30 "Et prosequitur usque in finem Praefationis, extensam tenens manum dexteram (quae extensio non est de valore)."—*Loc. cit.*

31 "De manus Extensione in Ordinatione Diaconali," *Periodica,* XL (1951), 264-270.

32 *Ibid.,* p. 267.

33 Cf. *supra,* p. 44.

34 Pujolras, "Annotationes," C.p.R.M., XXIX (1948), 10.

35 *Supra,* p. 45.

the valid administration of the sacrament.[36] By "moral contact" is meant an extension of the hand, apart from any bodily contact, above the head of the ordinand, but effected in such a manner that contact is virtually rather than actually accomplished. This concept, once proposed by St. Raymond of Peñafort,[37] had been rejected by the Sacred Congregation in their zeal for an absolutely safe norm for the validity of the sacrament.[38] The fact that the Holy Father declared that a "moral contact" suffices for validity is consistent with his intention that there by no occasions for doubts or scruples concerning the ordination. Therefore, the notion of "moral contact" can be interpreted with some degree of latitude. Any lowering of the hand of the bishop above the head of a specific candidate in such a way as to leave no doubt as to the intention of the bishop in the minds of those standing about would suffice for the validity of the ordination. On the other hand, one general imposition above the heads of several candidates would not be sufficient. Finally, the significance of the sacramental action would not be substantially affected if the bishop were to make the imposition with his left hand, or with both hands as in the ordination of a priest.[39]

In the former discipline the essential form of this Order was considered as consisting in the words which accompanied the imposition of the hand—*Accipe Spiritum Sanctum. . . .*[40] Now the essential form immediately follows this formulary, and is said after the imposition of the bishop's hand. Nevertheless, the moral union required between the matter and the form of the sacrament is easily seen, for the whole preface is constituted as the form of the sacrament, and the imposition takes place within the preface.

The very minimum that is required for the form "accepted and

[36] "Ne vero dubitandi praebeatur occasio, praecipimus ut impositio manuum in quolibet Ordine conferendo caput Ordinandi physice tangendo fiat, quamvis etiam tactus moralis ad sacramentum valide conficiendum sufficiat."—*AAS,* XL (1948), p. 7, n. 6.

[37] *Supra,* p. 32.

[38] *Supra,* p. 45.

[39] S.C.S. Off., 9 martii 1923—*Periodica,* XL (1951), 269.

[40] *Supra,* p. 46.

used by the Church" is that it signify the power of Orders and the grace of the Holy Spirit, which are the effects of the sacrament. In the esssential form of the Order of the diaconate the power of the Order is signified by the words *opus ministerii*, and the grace by the words *septiformis gratiae tuae munere roboretur.*[41] If either of these phrases were to be omitted from the form in its application, the sacrament would be essentially defective. Slight changes in the words of the form would, of course, not have this effect. In a case of doubt the Holy See should be consulted.

Of the remaining rites employed in the ordination of a deacon, only one is considered to be integral to the ordination according to the practice of the Roman Congregations. This is the ancient rite of the handing of the Book of the Gospels, symbolic of the power of the deacon to read and preach in the Church. If this rite is overlooked in the ordination, it should be supplied privately as soon as it can conveniently be done.

C. *The Priesthood*

Because of the greater number of rites added to the ceremony of ordination to the priesthood, more confusion existed in this Order than in any other. A proportionate number of problems called for a solution through the provisions of the Apostolic Constitution.

In the ordination of a priest the essential matter consists in the first imposition of hands made by the bishop in silence. The continuation of this action, which was designated as the second imposition of hands, is not included in the essential matter of the sacrament, nor is the third imposition of hands, which takes place after the second ablution. The form consists in the words of the preface, of which the following are essential and required for validity: *Da, quaesumus, Omnipotens Pater, in hunc famulum tuum Presbyterii dignitatem; innova in visceribus eius spiritum sanctitatis, ut acceptum a Te, Deus, secundi meriti munus obtineat censuramque morum exemplo suae conversationis insinuet.*[42]

[41] Damen, "In Constitutionem Apostolicam *Sacramentum Ordinis,*" *Euntes Docete,* I (1948), 110.

[42] "In Ordinatione Presbyterali materia est Episcopi prima manuum

The seeming separation of the matter from the form of the sacrament is more evident here than in the Order of the diaconate, since the imposition of the hands does not take place during the preface, but at the beginning of the ceremony. The whole tenor of the preface, however, suggests the reason for and the determination of the action of the bishop. This fact, as well as the total unity of purpose displayed in the ceremony of ordination, shows the intention of the ordaining prelate, and thus furnishes a sufficient moral unity for the matter and the form of the sacrament.[43]

For this reason nothing is accomplished by the seeking of a moral union for the matter and the form in the second imposition of the right hand of the bishop during the prayer *Oremus, Fratres carissimi,* or in the position of the bishop's hands during the preface. Neither action is required for the validity of the ordination; nor must they be supplied if they have been omitted, for they are classified as part of the rite of the imposition of hands, and not as a separate rite contributing to the integrity of the ceremony. Likewise, the revised rubric, in explaining the position of the bishop's hands during the recitation of the essential form,[44] adds nothing new to the ceremony, but simply clarifies what has always been the practice.

It is difficult to conceive of an error or a mistake in the first and necessary imposition of hands which would nullify the sacramental effect or bring it into doubt. Here, as in the ordination of a deacon, physical contact with the head of the ordinand in the imposition of hands is required for the lawful administration of the sacrament. A moral contact, however, is sufficient for the validity of the ordination. If the bishop were to impose only one hand, as in the ordination of a deacon, the effect of this action as a sensible sign productive of invisible grace would not

---

impositio quae silentio fit, non autem eiusdem impositionis per manus dexterae extensionem continuatio, nec ultima cui coniunguntur verba: 'Accipe Spiritum Sanctum: quorum remiseris peccata, etc.' Forma autem constat verbis 'Praefationis' quorum haec sunt essentialia ideoque ad valorem requisita: . . ."—*AAS,* XL (1948), n. 5.

[43] Hürth, "art. cit.," *Periodica,* XXXVII (1948), 30.

[44] ". . . extensis ante pectus manibus."

be lost, in the opinion of the writer. The words of the form would determine the application of the matter to the Order of the priesthood. Since the Constitution does demand the imposition of both hands of the bishop (*impositio manuum*), however, in the ordination of a priest, the facts should be presented to the Holy See for a judgment.

The essential form of the Order of the priesthood is governed by the same regulations that obtain in the conferring of the diaconate. The formula enunciated in the Constitution, and only this one, is "accepted and used by the Church" for the purpose of determining the application of the matter of the sacrament. These words express the giving of grace (*innova in visceribus eius spiritum sanctitatis*) and the conferring of power (*Presbyterii dignitatem*), which are the effects that must be produced and signified in an ordination to the priesthood.

If a change or omission of words were to result in the loss of the expression of either of these two ideas, the form would be substantially defective and the ordination invalid. Pope Leo XIII (1878-1903), in examining whether the Anglican Orders were valid, found them essentially defective on this point. The form used in the Edwardian Ordinal of 1552 reads: "Receive the Holy Ghost: whose sins thou dost forgive, they are forgiven; and whose sins thou dost retain, they are retained. And be thou a faithful dispenser of the Word of God and His holy sacraments." [45] This formula was held insufficient for giving expression to the power of offering sacrifice, which is essential to the priesthood.[46] The same principle is still applicable as a test of the validity of the sacramental formula, but with this difference. Since the Apostolic Constitution *Sacramentum Ordinis* became effective, these essential concepts—the conferring of power and grace—

[45] Stephens, *Anglican Orders* (Westminster, Md.: The Newman Press, 1956), p. 21.

[46] Leo XIII, litt. ap. *Apostolicae curae,* 13 sept. 1896, § 8: "Iamvero verba quae ad proximam usque aetatem habentur passim ab Anglicanis tamquam forma propria ordinationis presbyteralis, videlicet, *Accipe Spiritum Sanctum,* minime sane significant definite ordinem sacerdotii vel eius gratiam et potestatem, quae praecipue est potestas *consecrandi et offerendi verum corpus and sanguinem Domini,* eo sacrificio, quod non est *nuda commemoratio sacrificii in Cruce peracti.*"—*Fontes,* n. 631.

must be expressed in substantially the same formula as that prescribed by the Holy Father. Although other words could be found apt of themselves to express these ideas, the Holy Father specifically states that only the formulary accepted and used by the Church as the essential form suffices for the valid administration of the sacrament.[47]

Thus far only the essential rites of ordination to the priesthood have been considered. In effecting the repair of these rites, the minister must act in one of two ways: if the ordination is clearly defective, he must repeat the whole ceremony *ab initio;* if only doubtful, then he must present the circumstances of that ordination ceremony to the Holy See. Defects which occur in other parts of the ceremony never extend to the validity of the ordination, but only to the lawful application or procedure. Here the minister is obliged to repair the defective rites only if the integrity of the ordination is impaired.

A comparison of the ruling in the Apostolic Constitution with the former practice of the Roman Congregations establishes three individual rites within the ordination as integral parts of the whole ceremony. These are: The anointing of the hands of the newly ordained, which symbolizes the power to bless and to consecrate; the *traditio* of the chalice and the paten, symbolic of the power to offer the Holy Sacrifice of the Mass; the last imposition of the hands, which shows that the newly ordained has received the power to forgive sins. If one of these rites is omitted, the bishop is obliged to repair the defect as soon as he can conveniently do so, and in private. Only the specific action, together with the words which accompany it, are to be performed on this occasion.

Inasmuch as the tradition of the chalice and the paten is no longer even probably of the substance of the sacrament, certain prescriptions of the former discipline no longer apply.[48]

47 ". . formam vero itemque unam esse verba applicationem huius materia determinantia, quibus univoce significantur effectus sacramentales, —scilicet potestas Ordinis et gratia Spiritus Sancti,—quaeque ab Ecclesia qua talia accipiuntur et usurpantur."—*AAS,* XL (1948), p. 6, n. 4; Damen, "art cit.," *Euntes Docete,* I (1948), 109.

48 *Supra,* pp. 48-49.

Therefore, if the chalice used in the *traditio* was empty, or if it contained only water, or more water than wine, there would be no need to repeat the whole rite or any part of it, for the power to offer the sacrifice of the Mass would have been symbolized adequately apart from these elements. The same could be said if the host was missing from the paten. The words of the formula *Accipe potestatem offerre sacrificium Deo . . .* would determine that the handing over of the empty chalice or the empty paten was intended to signify the power to offer the sacrifice of the Mass. In the anointing of the hands and in the last imposition of hands the former prescriptions of the Holy See should be followed, except for one point. Formerly the final imposition of the hands was to be repeated if there was no physical contact with the newly ordained. In view of the regulations of the Apostolic Constitution this requirement no longer has any applicable force.

D. *The Episcopate*

Even before the issuance of the Apostolic Constitution *Sacramentum Ordinis* a certain unanimity of opinion existed among canonists and theologians as to the essential rites of consecration to the episcopate. Two facts especially were responsible for this harmony: The *Decretum pro Armenis* made no mention of the matter and the form of this Order, and Pope Leo XIII explicitly ruled out the formulary *Accipe Spiritum Sanctum* as the form of the sacrament.[49] Moreover, the Apostolic Constitution of 1944, entitled *Episcopalis Consecrationis*,[50] established beyond a doubt that the action of simply the one bishop consecrator was necessary for the validity of an episcopal consecration.

Therefore, the Apostolic Constitution of 1947 only made more precise what already was considered the common opinion of ecclesiastical writers. For the consecration to the episcopate the Holy Father decreed that the matter of the sacrament consists in the one imposition of the hands of the bishop consecrator, and that the form consists in the words of the preface, of which the following are essential: *Comple in Sacredote tuo ministerii*

[49] *Supra*, pp. 52-53.

[50] *AAS*, XXXVII (1945), 131-132.

tui summam, et ornamentis totius glorificationis instructum coelestis unguenti rore sanctifica.[51] In the application of the matter and the form of the sacrament the instructions contained in the Apostolic Constitution *Episcopalis Consecrationis* of November 30, 1944, are to be observed.

For the lawful administration of the sacrament in an episcopal consecration three ministers are required.[52] The first is the bishop-consecrator, who may be called the necessary minister of the episcopal consecration, for his action, and it alone, is required for the valid conferring of the sacrament. He is assisted by two bishops called the co-consecrators, who, having the intention of consecrating, actively co-operate with the necessary minister by imposing hands upon the candidate and saying all the prayers along with the consecrator, except the prayers for the blessing of the Pontifical vestments.[53] When two co-consecrators are not available, a dispensation must be sought.[54] In this case the Supreme Pontiff, in granting the dispensation, always commands that the consecrator be assisted by two or three priests of some special dignity.[55] These assisting priests cannot be designated as co-consecrators, for they are unable, as priests, to share the intention of the minister to consecrate. They should, however, follow in detail the directions of the Roman Pontifical in assisting the consecrator.[56]

The revised rubrics of the Roman Pontifical command that the ministers in applying the matter of the sacrament successively touch the head of the bishop-elect with both hands and say, each of them, as they impose hands, the formula, *Accipe*

[51] "Denique in Ordinatione seu Consecratione Episcopali materia est manuum impositio quae ab Episcope consecratore fit. Forma autem constat verbis 'Praefationis,' quorum haec sunt essentialia ideoque ad valorem requisita."—*AAS,* XL (1948), p. 7, n. 5.

[52] Canon 954.

[53] *AAS,* XXXVII (1945), 131.

[54] Canon 954.

[55] Cappello, *De Sacra Ordinatione,* n. 319.

[56] S.R.C., 9 iun. 1853—*Decr. Auth.,* n. 3014.

Spiritum Sanctum.[57] In this imposition of hands the co-consecrators together with the consecrator should act with the intention of conferring the episcopal consecration. If this imposition of hands is omitted by both the consecrator and the co-consecrators or their substitutes, the consecration is certainly invalid. If, however, only the consecrator imposes hands, and not the co-consecrators, then the conferring of the episcopal consecration is certainly valid. In this last case no repair of the rite or supply of the previously missing ceremony is needed, for the rite of the imposition of the hands is substantially complete.[58] The same is true if the imposition of the hands has been omitted by the consecrator, but performed by at least one of the co-consecrators. Here the consecration is valid, for all the conditions necessary for the valid conferring of the episcopal dignity are verified. It should be noted that the priest-assistants to the consecrator who act with papal dispensation effect nothing sacramental with their imposition of hands, but only complete or fill out the ceremony. The imposition of the hands must be performed by a bishop who recites the words of the form with the intention of consecrating. Thus, the Holy Father, in clarifying the office of the assisting bishops in an episcopal consecration has not only more clearly outlined the ceremonial functions of these co-consecrators, but has also made more certain the valid transfer of the Order of the episcopate.

The formula, *Accipe Spiritum Sanctum,* to be recited along with the imposition of hands, is not necessary to either the substance or the integrity of the consecration. Therefore, if it has been omitted it need not be supplied. The essential words of the form as found in the preface must, for the lawfulness of the consecration, be recited by all three of the ministers. The validity of the consecration is verified if any one of the three bishops who imposed hands by means of at least a moral contact pronounces the essential words of the form. If, for instance, one bishop alone said the words and another simply imposed hands the ordination would certainly be invalid. As in the other Orders,

[57] *Infra,* p. 110.

[58] Gasparri, *Tractatus Canonicus de Sacra Ordinatione,* n. 1001.

this form must not only univocally signify the power (*ministerii tui summam*) and the grace (*coelestis unguenti rore sanctifica*) of the sacrament,[59] but must also be the essential form used and accepted by the Church.[60]

Of the remaining rites employed in the consecration of a bishop, the imposition of the book on the neck and shoulders of the candidate together with the tradition of the book, and the anointing of the head and hands with oil, are, because of their antiquity and significance, to be honored as integral parts of the ceremony of consecration. This is in keeping with the practice developed before the Constitution. If the imposition of the book has been completely omitted, this action is to be supplied. If the omission of the imposition of the book is noted during the course of the ceremony, it can be supplied then. There is no formula of words accompanying this ritual action. In the event the tradition of the closed book of the gospels has been overlooked, this *traditio* should be supplied together with the prayer *Accipe Evangelium* which accompanies the ceremony.[61] The repair of the defective rites in the anointing of the hands and the head of the bishop follows the same regulations that obtained in the practice of the Roman Congregations prior to the Constitution.[62] Following the customary practice of the Roman Congregations would oblige the supply of the profession of faith by the bishop, if it should be omitted in the ceremony.[63]

Corollary: The Co-ministers in an Episcopal Consecration

While incidental reference has been made to the co-ministers in an episcopal consecration, the requirement as stated in canon 954, namely that two bishops assist in the lawful administering of the episcopal dignity, justifies a few additional words of comment. It was to establish with certitude the consecratory

[59] Damen, "art. cit.," *Euntes Docete,* I (1948), 110.

[60] Pujolras, "art. cit.," *C.p.R.M.*, XXIX (1948), 5.

[61] Many, *Praelectiones Canonicae de Sacra Ordinatione,* n. 297.

[62] *Supra,* pp. 51-54.

[63] *Supra,* p. 54.

function of these two bishops, formerly designated as "assistants," that Pope Pius XII issued his Apostolic Constitution *Episcopalis Consecrationis* of November 30, 1944.[64]

The use of more than one consecrator in an episcopal consecration belongs to the most ancient custom in the Church. Metropolitans consecrated their suffragans, and the patriarchs the metropolitans, in the presence of all the bishops of the province. As the Church grew and the assembling of all the bishops of the province became impossible, the custom arose of having at least three bishops co-operating in the consecration in the name of all the bishops of the province.[65] From the very dawn of this tradition each of the three bishops was considered as a consecrator.[66]

The rubrics of the Roman Pontifical before the recent revision were somewhat vague on this point. The assisting bishops were instructed to pronounce the words *Accipe Spiritum Sanctum* while touching the head of the bishop-elect, but for the remainder of the ceremony their duties seemed to be of an auxiliary character. Even while they read the remaining prayers with the consecrator, as the rubrics [67] and the authors [68] directed, there was no indication that they were to do so with the intention of consecrating. Moreover, the constant juxtaposition of the words *consecrator* and *assistentes* tended to foster the notion that there was but one true consecrator.

Actually the word *assistentes* was introduced into the ceremony

[64] The full text of the Constitution together with a translation into English will be found in the appendices of this work. *Infra,* pp. 96-99.

[65] Cf. Oppenheim, "Annotationes ad Constitutionem Appostolicam *Episcopalis Consecrationis,*" *Apollinaris* (Romae, 1928-), XIX (1946), 18-20.

[66] Franquesa, "La Constitucion Apostolica acerca de los Obispos Consagrantes," Revisita Española de Derecho Canonico (Salamanca, 1946-), II (1947), 237-238.

[67] "Assistentes vero Episcopi submissa voce dicunt quaecumque dixerit Consecrator, . . ."—*Pontificale Romanum, De Consecratione Electi in Episcopum.*

[68] Moretti, *Caeremoniale iuxta Ritum Romanum seu De Sacris Functionibus,* Vol. IV (Taurini: Marietti, 1939), nn. 2700, 2702; Martinucci-Menghini, *Manuale Sacrarum Caeremoniarum,* Pars II, Vol. II (Ratisbonae: Pustet, 1915), pp. 107, 111, 133, 138.

with the altogether opposite intention of bringing more clarity to the rite of consecration. Durantis of Mende, the father of the modern Pontifical, in attempting to specify more clearly the rôle of the consecrator bishop, used terms (*ductores, episcopi qui eum deduxerunt,* etc.) which had the effect of lessening the participation of the co-consecrators. Adalberto Franquesa, a monk of Montserrat, in his remarks on the development of this term *assistentes,* exonerates Durantis of any desire to introduce even indirectly any thought opposed to the tradition he inherited, but finds in the Pontifical of the Bishop of Mende the beginning of the false notion of the rôle of the co-consecrators, later characterized by the word *assistentes.*[69]

Perhaps the redactors of the first modern Pontifical under Pope Clement VIII should be held more responsible for the misunderstanding that was attached to the term under discussion, for, although they used the Pontifical of Durantis as a guide, they did not transfer to the new pontifical several rubrics, found in that Pontifical, which more clearly directed the co-consecrators to recite in a low voice all the prayers pronounced by the principal consecrator.[70]

The co-consecrators according to the revised rubrics of the Pontifical,[71] insofar as they are true consecrators, not only impose hands upon the bishop-elect, but likewise recite all the prayers recited by the principal consecrator, except those which are prescribed for the blessing of the pontifical vestments. Since they do this with the intention of consecrating, they confer, together with the consecrator, the sacrament of Orders. This rite can be numbered, then, with the concelebration performed at the Mass of priestly ordination and episcopal consecration as the only examples of the use of more than one minister in the confection of a sacrament in the Roman Rite. The co-consecrators, since they are ministers, are likewise obliged by the provisions of canon

[69] *Ibid.,* pp. 230-236.

[70] Before the preface Durantis listed the following rubric: "Deinde consecrator dicit voce mediocri, iunctis manibus ante pectus, et alii etiam episcopi, tenentes libros, idem dicunt voce submissa."—Andrieu, *Le Pontifical Romain au Moyen-Age,* III, 383.

[71] *Infra,* p. 109.

1002 to see that no change is made in the rites of episcopal consecration, and to effect any supply of rites that is demanded by law. With regard to the former obligation, the demands of the law affect all three consecrators equally; the principal consecrator, however, has the primary obligation with regard to the supply of any defective rites.

PART II

OTHER LEGAL REQUIREMENTS CONCERNING THE RITES AND CEREMONIES OF SACRED ORDINATION (CANONS 1003-1005)

CHAPTER 5

THE MASS OF ORDINATION OR CONSECRATION

ARTICLE I. THE MASS TO BE SAID

The proper time for ordination to both major and minor Orders is well established in law. Episcopal consecration must occur at Mass on a Sunday or on a day on which the death of an Apostle is commemorated. Major Orders must also take place at Mass. The ordinary days for the conferring of major Orders are the Ember Saturdays or the Saturday before the 1st Sunday of the Passion.[1] For a grave reason the bishop may confer these Orders on any Sunday or holy day of obligation. Although the Pontifical indicates that first tonsure and the minor Orders are to be given at Mass, the Code of Canon Law allows first tonsure to be given at any time; also the minor Orders are to be conferred on a Sunday or a feast of any class, in the morning, either within or outside of Mass.[2]

If the ordination or consecration takes place on a Sunday, on a day of precept, a feast of any class, or on any extraordinary day allowed by law or indult, the Mass to be celebrated is the Mass of the office of the day.[3]

Ordinations *extra tempora* in the United States are authorized by an indult first granted May 18, 1940. In an audience given

[1] The implementation of the restored *Ordo* for Holy Week has effected a change here in the Code of Canon Law. Holy Saturday or the Easter Vigil is no longer considered a proper time for the conferral of Orders. "Cum vigilia paschalis ad nativam sedem nocturnam restituta fuerit, non convenit, ut inter eiusdem Vigiliae Missarum solemnia, Tonsura vel Ordines minores aut maiores conferantur."—S.R.C., 1 febr. 1957. *AAS,* XLIX (1957), 95.

[2] Canon 1006, §§ 1-4; Cf. Reiss, *The Time and Place of Sacred Ordination* (The Catholic University of America Canon Law Studies, n. 343, Washington, D. C.: The Catholic University of America, 1957), pp. 48-56.

[3] S.R.C., 28 sept. 1675—Conte a Coronata, *De Sacramentis,* II, n. 200.

the Cardinal Prefect of the Sacred Congregation of the Sacraments, Pope Pius XII granted the faculty to the Bishops and Archbishops of this country to confer major Orders *"extra tempora a iure statuta scilicet diebus festis ritus duplicis primae vel secundae classis, quamvis non de praecepto, necnon nonnullis diebus sabbatis, exeunte anno scholari."* The faculty was granted for three years and has been renewed to the present time. The most recent renewal by Pope John XXIII was announced by the Apostolic Delegate in a letter dated December 28, 1960 (Prot. No. 249/40) and is effective until December 16, 1963. Three changes have occurred in the original rescript. The Apostolic Delegate in a letter dated May 6, 1949 states: "This concession will be in force until May 6, 1952, *in favor of all the local Ordinaries of this country* (italics added). The original Roman rescript granted the faculty to all Bishops and Archbishops of this country. Also, the words *"nonnullis sabbatis"* were changed to read *"ultimis sabbatis Maii et duobus primis sabbatis Junii, exeunte anno scholari. . . ."* The latest rescript (effective until December 16, 1963) reads: *"Ss. Ordinationes habendi extra tempora a iure statuta, scilicet diebus festis ritus primae vel secundae classis, quamvis non de praecepto, necnon ultimis sabbatis maii et duobus primis sabbatis iunii, iisdem causis perdurantibus."* The words *"ultimis sabbatis maii"* are generally understood to mean any Saturday which occurs in the calendar after the middle of the month of May.

If major or minor Orders are conferred on one of the appointed or ordinary Saturdays, however, the Mass is always of the Saturday, even if a feast of the 1st or 2nd class occurs.[4] The custom of substituting the Mass of the occurring feast on these days was expressly reprobated, even in cases wherein the ordination, for some good reason, was held privately.[5] In all the Masses of ordination the ritual prayer for the conferral of holy Orders is added under one conclusion to the collect of the Mass being said. All other collects except privileged commemorations are excluded.

Although it is fitting that Orders be conferred with great

[4] *AAS,* LII (1960), 648.

[5] S.R.C., *Fesulana,* 11 febr. 1764—*Decr. Auth.,* n. 2473, ad. 2.

solemnity, it is not necesary that the Mass of ordination be a solemn Pontifical Mass. The ordaining prelate may offer simply a low Mass. Indeed, because of the length of the ceremony, this practice has become more or less the rule. The provisions of canon 1006, § 2, namely that the ordination be given *intra Missarum solemnia* is completely susceptible to this interpretation.[6]

Article II. The Celebrant

The Mass of ordination or of episcopal consecration must always be celebrated by the minister of the ordination of the consecration himself.[7] When a candidate is raised to episcopal Orders, the Mass is said by the principal minister, the consecrator. The validity of the ordination or of the consecration would not in any way be affected if the Orders were conferred outside of the Mass, even though normally in an ordination to the priesthood and to the episcopate the subject and the minister concelebrate the Mass. The action would, however, be highly unlawful.

The gravity of the precept contained in canon 1003 springs from the fact that a most ancient custom existed in the Church with reference to this law. The Church simply never dispenses from this requirement, at least with reference to the three higher Orders.[8] The denial by the Congregation of Sacred Rites of a petition for such a dispensation may be cited as indicative of the attitude of the Congregation. A seventy-year-old bishop, afflicted with the infirmities which made it impossible for him to to say Mass or stand for a long period of time, asked for the faculty whereby some other dignitary in his diocese could allowably say the Mass of ordination while he, the diocesan episcopal ordinary, ordained from the *scamnum*.[9] Even under these circumstances his request was not granted.

[6] Reiss, *op. cit.,* p. 61; *contra,* Nabuco, *Pontificalis Romani Expositio Juridico-Practica* (3 vols., Petropoli, Brasilia: Sumptibus Editora Vozes Ltda., 1945), Vol. I, *De Personis,* n. 77.

[7] Canon 1003.

[8] Cappello remarks that Pope Pius X gave a certain bishop the faculty of conferring the subdiaconate outside the celebration of Mass in a particular case.—*De Sacra Ordinatione,* p. 419.

[9] S.R.C., *Vratislavien.,* die 8 iun. 1658.—*Fontes,* n. 5501.

The law extends to all Orders that are in fact conferred at Mass, even though the law does not demand that they be conferred during the Holy Sacrifice. Thus, if minor Orders were given apart from major Orders, but at Mass, the celebrant of the Mass would also have to be the minister of the ordination. Of course, minor Orders may be given immediately before or after Mass; here the minister and the celebrant could be two different persons.

Article III. The Reception of Holy Communion

Whenever an ordination takes place within Mass, it is customary for all the candidates for Orders to receive Holy Communion at that Mass. In this laudable custom the intimate relationship between Orders and the Eucharist is acknowledged, for each of the Orders borrows its importance and rank from the proximity which the exercise of the Orders affords in relation to the Eucharistic Sacrifice.

For those who are promoted to major Orders the reception of Holy Communion at the Mass of ordination is a matter of precept.[10] This is an altogether unusual requirement, for elsewhere, as in marriage, the reception of Communion is indeed encouraged, but never commanded. One reason for the law can be found in the tremendous obligations and duties assumed with the reception of sacred Orders, which duties the added grace of the Eucharist makes more easy of fulfillment.[11] Its origin, however, can be traced to the early Church, when the close association between the ordination of the Apostles and the institution of the Eucharist was maintained. Just as the Apostles received the sacrament from the hands of Our Lord, so the newly ordained ministers of the Church received the Body of Christ from the hands of the ordaining bishop.

In assessing the gravity of the obligation of receiving Holy Communion one must make the distinction between the Order of Priesthood on the one hand, and the Order of the Diaconate or also of the Subdiaconate on the other. In the former Order, the

[10] "Omnes ad maiores ordines promoti obligatione tenentur sacrae communionis in ipsa ordinationis Missa recipiendae."—Canon 1005.

[11] See the prayer *Hanc igitur,* said by the newly consecrated bishop at the Mass of consecration.

newly ordained celebrates the Mass of ordination with the ordaining prelate. Here the reception of Communion is necessary for the integrity of the sacrifice. Therefore, for the priest the obligation of receiving Holy Communion, though separate from the obligation of concelebrating the Mass, is gravely binding on that account. The obligation of the deacon or of the subdeacon, since this added factor is not involved, is enjoined only *sub levi* in the common opinion of authors.[12]

The newly consecrated bishop also concelebrates the Mass of Consecration together with his consecrator. He is certainly bound gravely on that account to communicate at the Mass of Consecration. He is not obliged, however, by canon 1005, for there only those who are promoted to major Orders are mentioned. In canon 949 only the priesthood, the diaconate and the subdiaconate are listed as falling under the designation of major or sacred Orders.

The manner of receiving Holy Communion also differs among the various Orders. The new priest approaches the bishop and, having kissed his ring, receives the small Host without any recited formula of prayers. The *Confiteor* is not sung, nor is the absolution given before the Communion of the newly ordained priest. The deacon and the subdeacon communicate in the accustomed manner, answering *Amen* to the prayer *Corpus Domini Nostri Jesu Christi custodiat te in vitam aeternam*. The same formula is used for the Communion of the newly tonsured and those ordained to the minor Orders.[13] It may be added here that the candidates for the episcopate and for the priesthood, inasmuch as they celebrate Mass, are bound to fast from solids for three hours, and from liquids for one hour, before the beginning of the Mass of ordination; the candidates for the other two major Orders may compute the length of time of their fast from the moment when Holy Comunion is to be received.

12 Regatillo, *Ius Sacramentarium* (2. ed., Santander: Sal Terrae, 1949), n. 922; Cappello, *De Sacra Ordinatione*, n. 558; Conte a Coronata, *De Sacramentis*, II, n. 201.

13 Cf. Stehle, *Manual of Episcopal Ceremonies* (4. ed., Latrobe, Pa.: The Archabbey Press, 1948), pp. 359-360.

CHAPTER 6

THE ORDINATION OF ORIENTALS IN THE LATIN RITE

Everywhere in the Code of Canon Law the juridic and ritual distinction between the Latin and the Oriental disciplines is rigorously observed. As concerns Orders, the proper Latin bishop is forbidden to ordain one of his own subjects of the Oriental rite.[1] Likewise it is not permissible for him to furnish dimissorial letters, in consequence of which his own Latin subjects might receive ordination from a bishop of another rite.[2] The privilege granted to some religious communities of sending their subjects to any bishop in communion with the Holy See for ordination is also circumscribed by the prohibition against any unauthorized admixture of rites.[3] In every case of this kind a special indult must be obtained from the Holy See.

Even with an indult the ordination of an Oriental candidate in the Latin rite presents a special difficulty when this person has already received some Order in his own rite. Most of the Churches of the East do not recognize or use the same number of minor Orders as are found in the Latin Church. To ordain an Oriental candidate to the next higher Order as delineated in his own rite could involve the omission of some of the minor Orders, a course strictly forbidden in canon 977.[4] When the Apostolic indult effects a temporary or a permanent change of rite the ordaining prelate is faced with the same problem of procedure. To solve this difficulty the law provides that the candidate, before being

[1] Canon 955, § 2.

[2] Canon 961.

[3] Regatillo, *Ius Sacramentarium,* n. 989.

[4] "Ordines gradatim conferendi sunt ita ut ordinationes per saltum omnino prohibeantur."

ordained to a higher Order, receive all the lesser Orders not yet received by him in the Oriental rite.[5]

Article I. The Apostolic Constitution *Etsi pastoralis*

The law of the Code as stated in canon 1004 was taken directly from a similar provision given to the Italo-Greek Church by Pope Benedict XIV (1740-1758). In his Apostolic Constitution *Etsi pastoralis* of May 26, 1742, the Pope recognized the problem presented in interritual ordinations and, in order to put to rest all doubts as to how the bishop should proceed, declared:

> If any cleric of the Greek rite, after being ordained a lector, has obtained from the Apostolic See an indult that major Orders may be conferred on him in the Latin rite, then, if this indult is obtained before the subdiaconate, he must first receive in the Latin rite the three minor Orders omitted (in his own rite). But if, beyond the Order of lector, he has been elevated to the subdiaconate in the Greek rite, and by dispensation the Apostolic faculty is granted to him in the same way of receiving the other Orders in the Latin rite, then, before his reception of the Order of the diaconate, only the Order of exorcist is to be supplied of the minor Orders, since through the subdiaconate conferred in the Greek rite the Orders of acolyte and ostiary are likewise considered as conferred. This same holds true of him who, along with the rest of the minor Orders, has received the diaconate or even the priesthood in the Greek Church, and afterwards is to be promoted to the holy Order of the priesthood, or of the episcopate respectively, in the Latin rite, by Apostolic indult: namely, the Order of exorcist must be supplied in these cases before the candidate is ordained as a priest, or consecrated as a bishop.[6]

[5] "Si quis, ritu orientali ad aliquos ordines iam promotus, a Sede Apostolica indultum obtinuerit superiores ordines suscipiendi ritu latino, debet prius ritu latino recipere ordines quos ritu orientali non receperit."—Canon 1004.

[6] § VII, n. 7: "Si quis ritu Graeco Clericus, et Lector tantum fuit initiatus, atque ex benignitate Sedis Apostolicae obtinuit, ut Maiores Ordines latinis caeremoniis sibi conferantur, is antequam Subdiaconus ordinetur, tres minores Ordines omissos debet ritu Latino suscipere. Si vero, praeter Lectoris Ordinem, ad Subdiaconatum etiam Graeco ritu ascendit, et ex dispensatione itidem Apostolica facultas sibi facta sit, caeteros Ordines rito Latino suscipiendi, antequam inter Diaconos cooptetur, ex minoribus

Since the present law of the Code makes no changes in the legislation of the Constitution *Etsi pastoralis,* but only extends its provisions to include all the Churches of the Oriental rite, canon 1004 must be interpreted in the light of the more detailed legislation of Pope Benedict XIV. Two points especially should be noted in this regard. The first concerns the extension of the words, *"ordines quos ritu orientali non receperit."* It is evident from the wording of the Constitution that the minor Orders in the Oriental rites need not be formally received to satisfy the requirements of the law; the virtual reception of the Order suffices. Thus the law is not so much interested in the supply of the ceremonies of the minor Orders as in the supply of the powers conveyed in these ceremonies. The second point concerns the phrase, *"superiores ordines."* The Constitution makes it quite clear that all the Orders are included here, even the episcopate.

Article II. Minor Orders in the Oriental Churches

The ancient discipline of the Oriental Churches with regard to minor Orders is found in the Council of Trullo (692). The sixth canon of that Council lists the cantor, the lector and the subdeacon among the minor Orders.[7] In general this same enumeration holds true in the present Oriental discipline, but the many shades of difference introduced especially through the influence of the Latin rite makes such a judgment falter badly when applied to the individual rites. The Order of cantor may be taken as an example. In some Churches it is equivalent to first tonsure, in others it is hardly distinguishable from the Order of Lector—since both Orders are given with the same ceremony—while in other Churches it is not even listed among the

---

Ordinibus Exorcistatum tantummodo supplere cogitur; cum per Subdiaconatum Graeco ritu collatum, Acolythatum, et Ostiariatum recepisse censeatur. Idem dicendum de eo, qui una cum reliquis inferioribus Ordinibus, Diaconatum, aut etiam Presbyteratum Graece suscepit, et Latino postea ritu ad Sacrum Presbyteratus respective Ordinem, aut Episcopatum promovendus sit, ex Apostolica concessione: nimirum Exorcistatus Ordinem in ipso, antequam Presbyter ordinetur, aut Episcopus consecretur, esse supplendum."—*Fontes,* n. 328.

[7] Bruns, *Canones Apostolorum et Conciliorum Saeculorum IV-VII* (2 vols., Berolini, 1839), I, 39.

minor Orders. The Order of cantor or psalmist, however, is of no direct interest in this study, for if it is not considered as first tonsure, it amounts to an additional minor Order which need not be taken into account with reference to a supplying of the missing Orders.

The Churches of the Oriental rite may be placed in three categories with reference to their use of minor Orders: Those which, like the Italo-Greek Church, follow the Byzantine discipline, those which follow the Latin discipline, and those which have a proper discipline of their own.

The discipline of the Ruthenian Church is typical of this first category.[8] Only two minor Orders are given—the lectorate and the subdiaconate—and these with simply a prayer and the imposition of the hands typical of the simple ordination ceremony of the Byzantine rite. The prayer used in the ordination to the subdiaconate, however, contains express mention of the duties attached to the Orders of acolyte and ostiary in the Latin Church.[9] Thus, according to the Constitution *Etsi pastoralis*, the Ruthenians and all the Churches that follow the Byzantine rite may be said to confer the Orders of acolyte and ostiary along with the Order of the subdiaconate. In addition to the Ruthenians, the following rites would adhere to this form of ordination: The Albanian, Bulgarian, Georgian, Greek, Italo-Greek, Melkite, and Rumanian Churches. The Alexandrian Copts must also be included in this category.[10]

[8] *Synodus Provincialis Ruthenorum, habita Zamosciae, a. 1720,* Tit. III, § 7, *De Sacris Ordinationibus—Acta et Decreta Sacrorum Conciliorum Recentiorum, Collectio Lacensis* (7 vols., Friburgi Brisgoviae, 1870-1892), II, 38 ff.

[9] The prayer of ordination reads: "Deus aeterne, qui reges unxisti, et Prophetas constituisti et consecrasti, et justus vocasti: Tu Domine, voca hunc servum tuum sancta vocatione in signo subdiaconatus, et elige eum, ut sit bonus minister Sanctae Ecclesiae tuae; largire ei domum Sancti tui Spiritus, et concede ei, Domine, ut amet communionem sacramentorum et decorum domus tuae, utque adstet januis sancti templi tui, et accendat lucernas domus orationis tuae, et cum timore ac sollicitudine et conscientia bona perficiat ministerium, ad quod eum vocasti, etc."—*Collectio Lacensis,* II, 243-244.

[10] *Synodus Alexandrina Coptorum* (Romae: Ex Typographia Polyglotta, 1898), p. 132.

Two Oriental Churches follow the Latin enumeration of the minor Orders. They confer the Orders of the ostiary, lector, exorcist and acolyte as minor Orders; subdeaconship is numbered among the major Orders. These two are the Armenian Church,[11] and the Malabar Church.[12] The individual Churches of the Chaldean rite follow this same enumeration, except that they list the Order of the subdiaconate with the minor Orders.[13] For the purpose of this study the Chaldeans, then, may be listed with the Armenians, and the Malabars.

Of the three remaining Churches, two, the Syro-Malankara Church [14] and the Ethiopian Church [15] have only the Orders of cantor, lector and subdeacon. The other three Orders are not mentioned as being even virtually contained in the subdiaconate.

The Syrian Church, with its own proper rites, is the final Church that must be considered. This Church lists three minor Orders: The psalmist or cantor, the lector and the subdeacon. As with the Churches which follow the Byzantine discipline, the minor Orders of ostiary and acolyte are virtually contained in the subdiaconate. The assertion is made also that the Order of cantor included not only the first tonsure as understood in the Latin Church, but also the Order of Exorcist.[16] There is no evi-

[11] *Acta et Decreta Concilii Nationalis Armenorum, Romae, a. 1911* (Romae, 1913), Caput IX, p. 253.

[12] *Synodus Diamperitana, a. 1599,* Actio VII, n. 158—Mansi, XXXV, 1275.

[13] *Les Actes du Synode Chaldeén célébré au Convent de Rabban Hormizd pres d'Alqoche du 7 au 21 juin, 1853—Codificazione Canonica Orientale, Fonti,* Serie I (Città del Vaticano: Typis Polyglottis Vaticanis, 1930-); *Fonti,* Serie II (Città del Vaticano: Typis Polyglottis Vaticanis, 1935-); *Fonti,* Serie III (Città del Vaticano: Typis Polyglottis Vaticanis, 1934-), Serie II, fasc. XVII (1942), 62 (hereafter cited *Fonti*).

[14] *De Fontibus Iuris Ecclesiastici Syro-Malankarensium,* Cap. VII, lib. 3. n. 203—*Fonti,* Ser. II, fasc. VIII (1937), 105-106.

[15] Guido, *Il Fetha Nagast* (Romae, 1899), Caput VII, p. 83.

[16] Art. XIII, 1, *De sacerdotio:* "Ordines minores in nostro ritu hi sunt; ordo psaltis seu cantoris, lectoratus et subdiaconatus. Ordo quidem psaltis continet primam tonsuram et exorcistatum Ecclesiae Romanae. Subdiaconatus autem continet ostiariatum et acolythatum Ecclesiae Romanae." —*Synodus Sciarfensis Syrorum, a. 1888* (Romae, 1896), pp. 132-133.

dence to that effect, however, in the prayer for the ordination of the cantor. No mention is made of the powers proper to the exorcist in the Roman rite;[17] nor is any reference made to this Order when the duties of the cantor are outlined.[18] The Order of exorcist, then, cannot be considered as given even virtually in the Syrian rite.

Article III. The Supplying of the Omitted Orders

Applying the substantive law interpreted in the light of the Apostolic Constitution *Etsi pastoralis* to the facts enumerated in the foregoing article, one may draw the following conclusions:

1. No supplying at all is necessary when members of the Armenian, the Malabar or the Chaldean rites continue to receive Orders in the Latin rite by indult.

2. In all the other Churches, when the indult is obtained after the subject has received the Order of lector in his own rite, the three Orders of ostiary, exorcist and acolyte must be supplied before the reception of the subdiaconate.

3. In these same Churches, if the indult is given after the subject has received the subdiaconate in his own rite, a distinction must be made. In the Churches of the Byzantine rite, in the Coptic Church and in the Syrian Church only the Order of exorcist must be supplied. In the Syro-Malankara and the Ethiopian Churches, not only the Order of Exorcist, but also the Order of ostiary and acolyte must be given. In either case the Orders must be supplied before the reception of the next higher Order, be it the diaconate, the priesthood or the episcopate.

[17] Cappello, *De Sacris Ordinationibus*, n. 730.

[18] *Synodus Sciarfensis Syrorum*, p. 142.

CONCLUSIONS

1. The present rites of sacred ordination reflect in their various parts the efforts of all the Churches of Western Christendom to enhance the solemnity and symbolism of the reception of Orders. Thes rites developed around the simple ceremony of the imposition of hands with the prayer of ordination which have been used in the Church from Apostolic times.

2. Canon 1002 incorporates in the Code of Canon Law all the requirements of liturgical law regarding the obligation of the minister in the act of ordination. Not the least of these is the obligation of the minister to repair defective rites.

3. All ordinations prior to April 28, 1948, must be judged in the light of the practice developed in the Sacred Congregations with reference to the repair of defective rites.

4. The Apostolic Constitution *Sacramentum Ordinis* did not abrogate all the practices of the earlier law, but mainly affected only those which pertain to the valid conferring of Orders.

5. In the ordination of a deacon, of a priest or of a bishop the necessary imposition of hands must be made by means of physical contact with the head of the ordinand for the lawfulness of the ordination.

6. The assisting bishops at an episcopal consecration are actually co-ministers along with the consecrator of the sacrament of Orders. They also guarantee the validity of the consecration when or if the consecrator acts invalidly.

7. In a supplying of the minor Orders which are lacking when a member of the Oriental rite receives a higher Order in the Latin rite, the minor Orders virtually received in the Oriental subdiaconate are considered as formally received.

APPENDIX I

CONSTITUTIO APOSTOLICA

De Duobus Qui Episcopali Consecrationi Adsunt[1]

PIUS EPISCOPUS
SERVUS SERVORUM DEI
AD PERPETUAM REI MEMORIAM

Episcopalis Consecrationis Ministrum esse Episcopum et ad huius Consecrationis validitatem unum solum sufficere Episcopum, qui cum debita mentis intentione essentiales ritus perficiat, extra omne dubium est diuturnaque praxi comprobatum. A priscis tamen Ecclesiae temporibus plures Episcopi huiusmodi Consecrationi adstiterunt, ac nostra quoque aetate "Pontificalis Romani" auctoritate praescribitur duo alii Episcopi Consecrationi adsint oportere, quamvis in perculiaribus rerum adiunctis a vetere instituto dispensatio concedatur, si Adsistentes haberi nequeant. Utrum vero qui adsunt Episcopi cooperatores et consecratores sint, an testes dumtaxat Consecrationis, non omnibus satis exploratum est eo vel magis quod "Pontificalis Romani" Rubricae, ubi de precibus recitandis agunt, saepe unum Consecratorem singulari numero innuunt, et manifeste non constat Rubricae praescriptionem, quae initio prostat ante Examen Electi —adsistentes videlicet Episcopos submissa voce dicere debere quaecumque dixerit Consecrator—ad universum pertinere totius Consecrationis ritum. Exinde factum est ut alicubi Episcopi adsistentes verbis "Pontificalis Romani" inhaerentes, prolatis verbis "Accipe Spiritum Sanctum" dum caput Electi cum Consecratore tangunt, postea ea quae sequuntur non pronuntient; alicubi vero, ut in Urbe, Episcopi non tantum praefata verba, sed submissa voce orationem quoque "Propitiare" cum sequenti Praefatione, quin etiam omnia et singula proferant quae Consecrator ab initio ad finem usque sacri ritus recitat vel canit.

Quibus omnibus diligentissime perpensis, eo consilio promoti ut Episcoporum, qui in Consecratione Electi ad Episcoparum adsunt, officio et ministerio provideatur et tam in Urbe quam in ceteris terrarum orbis partibus unus idemque semper agendi modus in posterum hac in re servetur, de Apostolicae plenitudine potestatis ea quae sequuntur declaramus, decernimus ad statuimus:

Licet ad Episcopalis Consecrationis validitatem unus tantummodo requiratur Episcopus idemque sufficiat, cum essentiales ritus perficiat, nihi-

[1] *AAS*, XXXVII (1945), 131-132.

APPENDIX I

THE APOSTOLIC CONSTITUTION

Concerning the Two Bishops Who Assist at an Episcopal Consecration

PIUS BISHOP
SERVANT OF THE SERVANTS OF GOD
FOR THE PERPETUAL REMEMBRANCE OF THE EVENT

It is beyond all doubt and proven by long-standing practice that the minister of an episcopal consecration is a bishop and that one bishop alone, who with the required intention of mind performs the essential rites, suffices for the validity of the consecration. From the earliest days of the Church, however, several bishops have assisted at a consecration of this kind, and also, in our own day, it is prescribed by the authority of the "Roman Pontifical" that two other bishops must be present at the consecration, although in extraordinary circumstances a dispensation is granted from this ancient institute if it is impossible to have Assisting Bishops. Nevertheless it is not sufficiently clear whether these bishops are present as cooperators and co-consecrators, or only as witnesses of the consecration, especially since the rubrics of the "Roman Pontifical," where they treat of the prayers to be recited, frequently indicate only one consecrator by using the singular number, and since it is not perfectly clear that the prescriptions of the rubrics given in the beginning of the ceremony before the examination of the bishop-elect—namely, that the assisting bishops are to say in a low voice whatever the consecrator says—applies to the entire rite of consecration.

Hence, it has happened that in some places the assisting bishops, following the instructions of the "Roman Pontifical," say only the words *Accipe Spiritum Sanctum* while touching the head of the bishop-elect, and do not pronounce the words which follow. Elsewhere, as in Rome, the assisting bishops not only say the aforementioned words, but also pronounce in a low voice the prayer *Propitiare* and the preface which follows, without, however, saying all the prayers to the end of the sacred rite.

Having given all these things careful thought, and being determined to establish the office and ministry of the bishops who are present at the consecration of the bishop-elect, so that henceforth both in Rome and in the rest of the world one and the same procedure should be observed in this matter, by the plenitude of Our Apostolic Powers, we declare, decree and establish the following:

Although, when the essential rites are performed, only one bishop is re-

lominus duo Episcopi, qui ex vetere instituto, secundum "Pontificalis Romani" praescriptum, adsunt Consecrationi, debent cum eodem Consecratore, et ipsi Consecratores effecti proindeque Conconsecratores deinceps vocandi, non solum utraque manu caput Electi tangere, dicentes "Accipe Spiritum Sanctum," sed, facta opportuno tempore mentis intentione conferendi Episcopalem Consecrationem una simul cum Episcopo Consecratore, orationem quoque "Propitiare" recitare cum integra sequenti Praefatione, itemque, universo ritu perdurante, ea omnia submissa voce legere quae Consecrator legit vel canit, exceptis tamen precibus ad pontificalium indumentorum benedictionem praescriptis, quae in ipso Consecrationis ritu sunt imponenda.

Quae autem hisce litteris Nostris declaravimus, decernimus, statuimus, ea omnia rata firmaque permanere auctoritate Nostra iubemus, quibuslibet minime obstantibus, perculiari etiam mentione dignis; proindeque volumus ac decernimus ut secundum data praescripta "Pontificale Romanum" opportune reformetur.

Nemini vero hanc paginam declarationis, decreti, statuti et voluntatis Nostrae infringere vel ei contraire liceat; si quis autem id ausu temerario attentare praesumpserit, indignationem omnipotentis Dei et Beatorum Apostolorum Petri et Pauli se noverit incursurum.

Datum Romae apud S. Petrum, anno Domini millesimo nongentesimo quadragesimo quarto, die trigesima Novembris mensis, in festo S. Andreae Apostoli, Pontificatus Nostri anno sexto.

Pius PP. XII

quired and suffices for the validity of an episcopal consecration, nevertheless, the two bishops who, from ancient custom and according to the prescription of the "Roman Pontifical," assist at the consecration—being themselves consecrators and thus henceforth to be called co-consecrators —should with the aforementioned consecrator not only touch the head of the elect with both hands and say *Accipe Spiritum Sanctum,* but, having made at an appropriate time the mental intention of conferring episcopal consecration together with the bishop consecrator, recite the prayer *Propitiare* with the entire preface that follows, and also, throughout the whole rite read in a low voice everything the consecrator reads or chants, except the prayers prescribed for the blessing of the pontifical vestments which are imposed in the rite of consecration.

We command that there remain fixed and sealed all these things which we have declared, decreed and ordained, all things to the contrary notwithstanding, even such as are worthy of special mention; accordingly we wish and prescribe that the "Roman Pontifical" be revised in conformity with the foregoing demands.

Let no one regard it permissable to go contrary to or to infringe upon this written declaration, decree statute or manifestation of our will; if anyone seeks with presumptions and temerarious intent to do so, let him realize that he will incur the indignation of God Almighty and the Blessed Apostles Peter and Paul.

Given at St. Peter's in Rome, November 30, 1944, on the feast of St. Andrew, in the sixth year of Our Pontificate.

Pope Pius XII

APPENDIX II

CONSTITUTIO APOSTOLICA

De Sacris Ordinibus Diaconatus, Presbyteratus et Episcopatus [1]

PIUS EPISCOPUS
SERVUS SERVORUM DEI
AD PERPETUAL REI MEMORIAM

1. Sacramentum Ordinis a Christo Domino institutum, quo traditur spiritualis potestas et confertur gratia ad rite obeunda munia ecclesiastica, unum esse idemque pro universa Ecclesia, catholica fides profitetur; nam sicut Dominus Noster Iesus Christus Ecclesiae non dedit nisi unum idemque sub Principe Apostolorum regimen, unam eandemque fidem, unum idemque sacrificium, ita non dedit nisi unum eundemque thesaurum signorum efficiacium gratiae, id est Sacramentorum. Neque his a Christo Domino institutis Sacramentis Ecclesia saeculorum cursu alia Sacramenta substituit vel substituere potuit, cum, ut Concilium Tridentium docet (Conc. Trid., Sess. VII, can. 1, *De Sacram. in genere*), septem Novae Legis Sacramenta sint omnia a Iesu Christo Domino Nostro instituta et Ecclesiae nulla competat potestas in "substantiam Sacramentorum," id est in ea quae, testibus divinae revelationis fontibus, ipse Christus Dominus in signo sacramentali servanda statuit.

2. Quod autem ad Sacramentum Ordinis de quo agimus spectat, factum est ut, non obstante eius unitate et identitate, quam nemo unquam e catholicis in dubium revocare potuit, tamen aetatis progressu, pro temporum et locorum diversitate, illi conficiendo ritus varii adiicerentur; quod profecto ratio fuit cur theologi inquirere coeperint, quinam ex illis in ipsius Sacramenti Ordinis collatione pertineant ad essentiam, quinam non pertineant: itemque causam praebuit dubiis et anxietatibus in casibus particularibus, ac propterea iterum ab Apostolica Sede humiliter expostulatum fuit, ut tandem quid in Sacrorum Ordinum collatione ad validitatem requiratur, suprema Ecclesiae auctoritate decerneretur.

3. Constat autem inter omnes Sacramenta Novae Legis, utpote signa sensibilia atque gratiae invisibilis efficientia, debere gratiam et significare

[1] *AAS,* XL (1948), 5-7.

APPENDIX II

THE APOSTOLIC CONSTITUTION

Concerning the Sacred Orders of the Diaconate, the Priesthood, and the Episcopate

PIUS BISHOP
SERVANT OF THE SERVANTS OF GOD
IN ABIDING MEMORY OF THE EVENT

1. The Catholic Faith professes that the sacrament of Orders instituted by Christ Our Lord, by which spiritual power is given and grace is conferred for the proper performance of ecclesiastical functions, is one and the same for the universal Church; for just as Our Lord Jesus Christ gave the Church one and the same government under the Prince of the Apostles, one and the same faith, and one and the same sacrifice, so He also gave the Church one and the same treasury of the efficacious signs of grace, namely, the sacraments. And the Church has not in the course of time substituted other sacraments in place of the sacraments instituted by Christ Our Lord—nor could She do so—since, as the Council of Trent teaches (Conc. Trid., Sess. VII, can. 1, *De Sacram. in genere*), the seven sacraments of the New Law were all instituted by Our Lord Jesus Christ, and the Church has no power over the "substance of the sacraments," that is, over those things which, as the sources of divine revelation bear witness, Christ the Lord Himself set up for observance in the sacramental sign.

2. Regarding the sacrament of Orders about which we are speaking, it is true that, notwithstanding its unity and identity, which no Catholic has even been able to question, in the course of time various rites have been added to its conferring, according to the diverse conditions of time and place. This was doubtless the reason why theologians began to inquire which of these rites as used in the conferring of the sacrament of Orders pertain to its essence and which do not; this also gave rise to doubts and anxieties in particular cases, and therefore time and time again the request has been humbly directed to the Apostolic See that those things which are required for the valid conferring of the sacrament of Orders should be declared by the supreme authority of the Church.

3. It is apparent to all that the sacraments of the New Law, inasmuch as they are sensible signs and produce invisible grace, must both signify the

quam efficiunt et efficere quam significant. Iamvero effectus, qui Sacra Diaconatus, Presbyteratus et Episcopatus Ordinatione produci ideoque significari debent, potestas scilicet et gratia, in omnibus Ecclesiae universalis diversorum temporum et regionum ritibus sufficienter significati inveniuntur manuum impositione et verbis eam determinantibus. Insuper nemo est qui ignoret Ecclesiam Romanam semper validas habuisse Ordinationes graeco ritu collatas absque instrumentorum traditione, ita ut in ipso Concilio Florentino, in quo Graecorum cum Ecclesia Romana unio peracta est, minime Graecis impositum est, ut ritum Ordinationis mutarent vel illi instrumentorum traditionem insererent: immo voluit Ecclesia ut in ipsa Urbe Graeci secundum ritum ordinarentur. Quibus colligitur, etiam secundum mentem ipsius Concilii Florentini, traditionem instrumentorum non ex ipsius Domini Nostri Iesu Christi voluntate ad substantiam et ad validitatem huius Sacramenti requiri. Quod si ex Ecclesiae voluntate et praescripto eadem aliquando fuerit necessaria ad valorem quoque norunt Ecclesiam quod statuit etiam mutare et abrogare valere.

4. Quae cum its sint, divino lumine invocato, suprema Nostra Apostolica Auctoritate et certa scientia declaramus et, quatenus opus sit, decernimus et disponimus: Sacrorum Ordinum Diaconatus, Presbyteratus et Episcopatus materiam eamque unam esse manuum impositionem; formam vero itemque unam esse verba applicationem huius materiae determinantia, quibus univoce significantur effectus sacramentales,—scilicet potestas Ordinis et gratia Spiritus Sancti,—quaeque ab Ecclesia qua talia accipiuntur et usurpantur. Hinc consequitur ut declaremus, sicut revera ad omnem controversiam auferendam et ad conscientiarum anxietatibus viam praecludendam, Apostolica Nostra Auctoritate declaramus, et, si unquam aliter legitime dispositum fuerit, statuimus instrumentorum traditionem saltem in posterum non esse necessariam ad Sacrorum Diaconatus, Presbyteratus et Episcopatus Ordinem validatatem.

5. De materia autem et forma in uniuscuiusque Ordinis collatione, eadem suprema Nostra Apostolica Auctoritate, quae sequuntur decernimus et constituimus: In Ordinatione Diaconali materia est Episcopi manus impositio quae in ritu istius Ordinationis una occurrit. Forma autem constat verbis "Praefationis" quorum haec sunt essentialia ideoque ad valorem requisita: "*Emitte in eum, quaesumus, Domine, Spiritum Sanctum, quo in opus ministerii tui fideliter exsequendi septiformis gratiae tuae munere roboretur.*" In Ordinatione Presbyterali materia est Episcopi prima manuum impositio quae silentio fit, non autem eiusdem impositionis per manus dexterae extensionem continuatio, nec ultima cui coniunguntur

grace which they effect and effect that which they signify. Now the effects which must be produced and correspondingly signified in sacred ordination to the diaconate, the priesthood and the episcopate, namely power and grace, have been found to be sufficiently signified, in all the rites used at different times and in various places in the universal Church, through the imposition of hands and the words determining this action. Furthermore, everyone knows that the Roman Church has always held as valid the ordinations conferred in the Greek rite apart from the *traditio instrumentorum,* so much so that in the very Council of Florence, in which the Greeks were brought into union with the Roman Church, no demand was made of the Greeks that they change their rite of ordination or include in it the *traditio instrumentorum:* nay more, the Church wished that the Greeks should ordain according to their own proper rite in the city of Rome itself. It follows that, even according to the mind of the Council of Florence itself, the *traditio instrumentorum* was not required from the will of Our Lord Jesus Christ for the essence and the validity of the sacrament. If, however, this was at one time required for validity from the will and the prescription of the Church, all know that what the Church establishes She can also change or abrogate.

4. Since this is true, we, after having asked for divine guidance, declare by Our Supreme Apostolic Authority and with certain knowledge, and, insofar as it is necessary, decree and provide that the one and sole matter of the Sacred Orders of the Diaconate, of the Priesthood and of the Episcopate is the imposition of hands, and likewise that the one and only form consists in the words which determine the application of this matter, by which are univocally signified the sacramental effects which as such —namely the power of Orders and the grace of the Holy Spirit—are accepted and employed by the Church. Hence it follows that We should speak with authority concerning this matter, as in fact in order to dispel all controversy and to close the door to all anxieties of conscience we do, by Our Apostolic Authority, declare, and, if ever any other legitimate provision was made to the contrary, establish that, at least for the future, the *traditio instrumentorum* is not necessary for the valid conferring of the Sacred Orders of the Diaconate, the Priesthood and the Episcopate.

5. Regarding the matter and the form used in the conferring of each of the Orders, We, by the same Apostolic Authority, ordain and decree the following: In the ordination of a deacon the matter is the imposition of the hand of the bishop, which occurs once in this rite of ordination. The form consists in the words of the "preface," of which these are essential and therefore required for validity: "*Emmite in eum, quaesumus, Domine, Spiritum Sanctum, quo in opus ministerii tui fideliter exsequendi septiformis gratiae tuae munere roboretur.*" In the ordination of a priest the matter is the first imposition of the hands of the bishop, which is done in silence, not the continuation of this imposition through the extension of the right hand, nor the last imposition, to which are joined the words:

verba: "Accipe Spiritum Sanctum: quorum remiseris peccata, etc." forma autem constat verbis "Praefationis" quorum haec sunt essentialia ideoque ad valorem requisita: "*Da, quaesumus, omnipotens Pater, in hunc famulum tuum Presbyterii dignitatem; innova in visceribus eius spiritum sanctitatis, ut acceptum a Te, Deus, secundi meriti munus obtineat censuramque morum exemplo suae conversationis insinuet.*" Denique in Ordinatione sue Consecratione Episcopali materia est manuum impositio quae ab Episcopo consecratore fit. Forma autem constat verbis "Praefationis," quorum haec sunt essentialia ideoque ad valorem requisita: "*Comple in Sacerdote tuo ministerii tui summam, et ornamentis totius glorificationis instructum coelestis unguenti rore sanctifica.*" Omnia autem haec fiant sicut per Apostolicam Nostram Constitutionem "Episcopalis Consecrationis" diei trigesimi novembris anni 1944 statutum est.

6. Ne vero dubitandi praebeatur occasio, praecipimus ut impositio manuum in quolibet Ordine conferendo caput Ordinandi physice tangendo fiat, quamvis etiam tactus moralis ad Sacramentum valide conficiendum sufficiat.

Tandem quae supra de materia et forma declaravimus ac statuimus, nequaquam ita intelligere fas sit ut vel paulum negligere vel praetermittere liceat ceteros "Pontificalis Romani" ritus constitutos; quin immo iubemus ut omnia data praescripta ipsius "Pontificalis Romani" sancte serventur et perficientur.

Huius Nostrae Constitutionis dispositiones vim retroactivam non habent; quod si dubium aliquod contingat, illud huic Apostolicae Sedi erit subiiciendum.

Haec edicimus, declaramus et decernimus, quibuslibet non obstantibus, etiam speciali mentione dignis, proindeque volumus et iubemus ut eadem in "Pontificali Romano" quadam ratione evidentia fiant. Nulli igitur homini liceat hand Constitutionem a Nobis latam infringere vel eidem temerario ausu contraire.

Datum Romae, apud Sanctum Petrum, die trigesimo novembris, in festo S. Andreae Apostoli, anno millesimo nongentesimo quadragesimo septimo, Pontificatus Nostri nono.

Pius PP. XII

"Accipe Spiritum Sanctum: quorum remiseris peccata, etc." The form consists in the words of the "preface," of which these are essential and therefore required for validity: "*Da, quaesumus, omnipotens Pater, in hunc famulum tuum Presbyterii dignitatem; innova in visceribus eius spiritum sanctitatis, ut acceptum a Te, Deus, secundi meriti manus obtineat censuramque morum exemplo suae conversationis insinuet.*" Finally, in the ordination or consecration of a bishop the matter is the imposition of the hands which is done by the bishop consecrator. The form consists in the words of the "preface," of which the following are essential and therefore required for validity: "*Comple in Sacerdote tuo ministerii tui summam, et ornamentis totius glorificationis instructum coelestis unguenti rore sanctifica.*" All of these things are to be done as was determined by Our Apostolic Constitution *Episcopalis Consecrationis* of November 30, 1944.

6. In order that no future occasion for doubt may arise, We command that the imposition of hands as used in the conferring of any and every Order be accomplished by means of a physical touching of the head of the one to be ordained, although even a moral contact is sufficient for the valid conferring of the sacrament.

Finally, those things which We have above declared and established regarding the matter and the form are not to be understood in such a way as to make it allowable for the other rites as prescribed in the Roman Pontifical to be neglected or passed over even in the slightest detail; nay rather We order that all the prescriptions contained in the Roman Pontifical itself be faithfully observed and performed.

The provisions of this Our Constitution do not have retroactive force, but if any doubt does arise, it should be submitted to this Apostolic See.

These things We proclaim, declare and ordain, all things, even such as deserve special mention, notwithstanding, and accordingly We desire and command that in some way these things be made evident in the Roman Pontifical. Let no man therefore infringe this Conistitution which We have given, or rashly dare to contravene the same.

Given in Rome, at St. Peter's, on the thirtieth day of November, the Feast of St. Andrew the Apostle, in the year nineteen hundred and forty-seven, the ninth year of Our Pontificate.

Pope Pius XII

APPENDIX III

THE DECREE OF THE SACRED CONGREGATION OF RITES CONCERNING THE CHANGES IN THE RUBRICS OF THE ROMAN PONTIFICAL[1]

SACRA CONGREGATIO RITUUM

URBIS ET ORBIS

DECRETUM

Edita a Sanctissimo Domino Nostro Pio XII Apostolica Constitutione *Sacramentum Ordinis* die 30 Novembris anno 1947 (A.A.S., 1948, p. 5), in qua determinatur forma sacramentalis Ordinum: Diaconatus, Presbyteratus et Episcopatus, Sacra Rituum Congregatio, pontificio mandato obsequens, variationes atque addenda in rubricis Pontificalis Romani, necnon rationem qua sacramentales formae sunt typis edendae, ut evidentiores fiant, disposuit, atque mandat ut haec in novis Pontificalis Romani editionibus inserantur; interim vero in folio separato edantur in Episcoporum commodum, ea ratione qua in annexis foliis continetur. Contrariis quibuscumque minime obstantibus.

Datum Romae, die 20 Februarii 1950.

✠ C. Card. Micara, Ep. Velitern., *Prefectus.*

✠ A. Carinci, Archiep. Seleucien., *Secretarius.*

VARIATIONES IN RUBRICIS PONTIFICALIS ROMANI

PARS I

CAPUT II

De Ordinibus conferendis

In Rubricis generalibus, ante collationem Sacrorum Ordinum positis, deleantur hæc verba:

"Moneat ordinandos, quod instrumenta, in quorum traditione character imprimitur, tangant."

[1] *AAS,* XLII (1950), 448-455.

De Ordinatione Diaconi

Omnia ut in Pontificali Romano usque ad Præfationem.

Præfatio

Per ómnia sæcula sæculórum.
℟. Amen.
℣. Dóminus vobíscum.
℟. Et cum spíritu tuo.
℣. Sursum corda.
℟. Habémus ad Dóminum.
℣. Grátias agámus Dómino Deo nostro.
℟. Dignum et justum est.

Vere dignum et justum est, æquum et salutáre, nos tibi semper et ubíque grátias ágere: Dómine sancte, Pater omnípotens, ætérne Deus, honórum dator, ordinúmque distribútor, atque officiórum dispósitor, qui in te manens ínnovas ómnia, et cuncta dispónis per verbum, virtútem, sapientiámque tuam, Jesum Christum Fílium tuum Dóminum nostrum, sempitérna providéntia præparas, et síngulis quibúsque tempóribus aptánda dispénsas. Cujus corpus, Ecclésiam vidélicet tuam, cæléstium gratiárum varietáte distínctam, suorúmque connéxam distinctióne membrórum, per legem mirábilem totíus compáginis unítam, in augméntum templi tui créscere, dilataríque largíris: sacri múneris servitútem trinis grádibus ministrórum nómini tuo militáre constítuens; eléctis ab inítio Levi fíliis, qui in mýsticis operatiónibus domus tuæ fidélibus excúbiis permanéntes, hæreditátem benedictiónis ætérnæ sorte perpétua possidérent. Super hos quoque fámulos tuos, quæsumus, Dómine, placátus inténde, quos tuis sacris altáribus servitúros in offícium Diaconátus supplíciter dedicámus. Et nos quidem tamquam hómines, divíni sensus et summæ ratiónis ignári, horum vitam, quantum póssumus, æstimámus. Te autem, Dómine, quæ nobis sunt ignóta non tránseunt, te occúlta non fallunt. Tu cógnitor es secretórum: tu scrutátor es córdium. Tu horum vitam cælésti póteris examináre judício, quo semper prævales, et admíssa purgáre et ea, quæ sunt agénda, concédere.

Hic solus Pontifex, manum dexteram extendens, ponit super caput cuilibet ordinando, dicens cuilibet, sine cantu:

Accipe Spíritum Sanctum, ad robur, et ad resisténdum diábolo, et tentatiónibus ejus. In nómine Dómini.

Postea, extensam tenens manum dexteram, dicit verba formæ sacramentalis, sine cantu:

Emítte in eos, quæsumus, Dómine, Spíritum Sanctum, quo in opus ministérii tui fidéliter exsequéndi septifórmis grátiæ tuæ múnere roboréntur.

Et prosequitur usque in finem Præfationis, extensam tenens manum dexteram (quae extensio non est de valore):

Abúndet in eis totíus forma virtútis, auctóritas modésta, pudor constans, innocéntiæ púritas, et spirituális observántia disciplínæ. In móribus eórum præcépta tua fúlgeant; ut suæ castitátis exémplo imitatiónem sanctam plebs acquírat: et bonum consciéntiæ testimónium præferéntes, in Christo firmi et stábiles persevérent; dignísque succéssibus de inferióri gradu per grátiam tuam cápere potióra mereántur.

Quod sequitur, dicit submissa voce legendo, ita tamen quod a circumstantibus possit audiri.

Per eúmdem Dóminum nostrum Jesum Christum Fílium tuum: Qui tecum vivit et regnat in unitáte ejúsdem Spíritus Sancti Deus, per ómnia sæcula sæculórum.

℟. Amen.

Post hæc Pontifex, sedens cum mitra, cuilibet ordinato ante se genuflexo stolam, quam singuli in manu habent, imponit, successive super humerum sinistrum, dicens singulis:

Accipe stolam cándidam, etc. . .

Cetera quæ sequuntur ut in Pontificali Romano.

De Ordinatione Presbyteri

Omnia ut in Pontificali Romano usque ad Præfationem.

Præfatio

Per ómnia sæcula sæculórum.
℟. Amen.
℣. Dóminus vobíscum.
℟. Et cum spíritu tuo.
℣. Sursum corda.
℟. Habémus ad Dóminum.
℣. Grátias agámus Dómino Deo nostro.
℟. Dignum et justum est.

Vere dignum et justum est, æquum et salutáre, nos tibi semper et ubíque grátias ágere: Dómine sancte, Pater omnípotens, ætérne Deus, honórum auctor et distribútor ómnium dignitátum; per quem profíciunt univérsa, per quem cuncta firmántur, amplificátis semper in mélius natúræ rationális increméntis, per órdinem cóngrua ratióne dispósitum. Unde et Sacerdotáles gradus, atque offícia Levitárum, Sacraméntis mýsticis institúta crevérunt: ut cum Pontífices summos regéndis pópulis præfecísses, ad eórum societátis et óperis adjuméntum, sequéntis órdinis viros et secúndæ dignitátis elígeres. Sic in erémo per septuagínta virórum prudéntium mentes, Móysi spíritum propagásti; quibus ille adjutóribus usus, in pópulo innúmeras multitúdines fácile gubernávit. Sic et Eleázarum et Ithamárum filios Aaron patérnæ plenitúdinis abundántiam transfudísti; ut ad hóstias salutáres, et frequentióris offícii Sacraménta, ministérium suffíceret Sacerdótum. Hac providéntia, Dómine, Apóstolis Fílii tui Doctóres fídei cómites addidísti, quibus illi orbem totum secúndis prædicatiónibus implevérunt. Quaprópter infirmitáti quoque nostræ, Dómine, quæsumus, hæc adjuménta largíre; qui quanto fragilióres sumus, tanto his plúribus indigémus.

Postea dicit verba formæ sacramentalis, quæ dici debet sine cantu, extensis ante pectus manibus:

Da, quæsumus, omnípotens Pater, in hos fámulos tuos presbytérii dignitátem; ínnova in viscéribus eórum spíritum sanctitátis; ut accéptum a te, Deus, secúndi mériti munus obtíneant, censurámque morum exémplo suæ conversatiónis insínuent.

Et prosequitur cum cantu:

Sint próvidi cooperatóres órdinis nostri; elúceat in eis totíus forma justítiæ, ut bonam ratiónem dispensatiónis sibi créditæ redditúri, ætérnæ beatitúdinis præmia consequántur.

Quod sequitur, legat submissa voce, ita tamen quod a circumstantibus audiri possit.

Per eúmdem Dóminum nostrum Jesum Christum Fílium tuum: Qui tecum vivit et regnat in unitáte ejúsdem Spíritus Sancti Deus, per ómnia sæcula sæculórum.
℟. Amen.

Cetera quæ sequuntur ut in Pontificali Romano, mutatis tamen quibusdam Rubricis, ut sequitur:

Intonato Hymno "Veni Creátor" ponatur hæc Rubrica:

Surgit Pontifex, et facit ut in fine Hymni habetur, interim schola prosequitur Hymnum: qui, si propter ordinatorum multitudinem necesse fuerit, repetatur, omisso primo Versu.

In Rubrica posita post Hymnum, loco illorum verborum: ". . . et singuli ordinandi successive . . . ," ponantur hæc verba:

". . et singuli ordinati successive . . ."

Rubrica posita post manuum unctionem sic immutetur:

"Pontifex producit manu dextera signum crucis super manum ordinati, et prosequitur:"

Et in fine formulæ unctionis ponatur:

"Et quilibet ordinatus respondeat: Amen."

De Consecratione Episcopi

Ubicumque in Rubricis occurrunt verba "Episcopi Assistentes" legatur: *"Episcopi Conconsecrantes."*

Immediate ante Præfationem, Rubricæ "Deinde Consecrator et Assistentes Episcopi . . ." hæc alia substituatur:

Deinde Consecrator ambabus manibus caput Consecrandi tangit, dicens: "Accipe Spíritum Sanctum," *quod successive faciunt Episcopi Conconsecrantes, qui non solum debent utraque manu caput Electi tangere, dicentes:* "Accipe Spíritum Sanctum," *verum etiam, facta opportuna tempore mentis intentione conferendi episcopalem consecrationem una simul cum Episcopo Consecratore, orationem quoque* "Propitiáre" *recitare cum integra sequenti Præfatione, itemque, universo ritu perdurante, ea omnia submissa voce legere quæ Consecrator legit vel canit, exceptis tamen precibus ad pontificalium indumentorum benedictionem præscriptis, quæ in ipso Consecrationis ritu sunt imponenda.*

Quo facto, Consecrator stans, deposita mitra, dicit:

Propitiáre, Dómine, supplicatiónibus nostris, et inclináto super hunc fámulum tuum cornu grátiæ sacerdotális, bene✠dictiónis tuæ in eum effúnde virtútem. Per Dóminum nostrum Jesum Christum Fílium tuum: Qui tecum vivit et regnat in unitáte Spíritus Sancti Deus:

Deinde extensis manibus ante pectus, dicit:

Per ómnia sæcula sæculórum.
℟. Amen.
℣. Dóminus vobíscum.
℟. Et cum spíritu tuo.
℣. Sursum corda..
℟. Habémus ad Dóminum.
℣. Grátias agámus Dómino Deo nostro.
℟. Dignum et justum est.

Vere dignum et justum est, æquum et salutáre, nos tibi semper et ubíque grátias ágere: Dómine sancte, Pater omnípotens, ætérne Deus, honor ómnium dignitátum, quæ glóriæ tuæ sacris famulántur ordínibus. Deus, qui Móysen fámulum tuum secréti familiáris affátu, inter cétera cæléstis documénta cultúræ, de hábitu quoque induménti sacerdotális instítuens, eléctum Aaron mýstico amíctu vestíri inter sacra jussísti, ut intelligéntiæ sensum de exémplis priórum cáperet secutúra postéritas, ne erudítio doctrínæ tuæ ulli deésset ætáti. Cum et apud véteres reveréntiam ipsa significatiónum spécies obtinéret, et apud nos certióra essent experiménta rerum, quam ænígmata figurárum. Illíus namque Sacerdótii anterióris hábitus, nostræ mentis ornátus est, et Pontificálem glóriam non jam nobis honor comméndat véstium, sed splendor animárum. Quia et illa, quæ tunc carnálibus blandiebántur obtútibus, ea pótius quæ in ipsis erant, intelligénda poscébant. Et idcírco huic fámulo tuo quem ad summi Sacerdótii ministérium elegísti, hanc, quæsumus, Dómine, grátiam largiáris, ut quidquid illa velámina in fulgóre auri, in nitóre gemmárum, et in multímodi óperis varietáte signábant, hoc in ejus móribus actibúsque claréscat.

Postea dicit verba formæ consecrationis episcopalis, quæ dici debent sine cantu, extensis ante pectus manibus:

Comple in sacerdóte tuo ministérii tui summam, et ornaméntis totíus glorificatiónis instrúctum, cæléstis unguénti rore sanctífica.

Si in Curia Romana fit Consecratio, Subdiaconus Apostolicus, vel unus ex Capellanis Pontificis ligat caput Consecrati cum una ex longioribus mappulis de octo superius dictis, et Consecrator, flexis genibus, versus ad altare incipit, ceteris prosequentibus, Hymnum:

Veni, Creátor Spíritus,

et dicitur usque ad finem, prout habetur supra in Ordinatione Presbyteri.

Finito primo versu, surgit Pontifex; et sedet in faldistorio ante medium altaris; capit mitram; deponit annulum et chirothecas; resumit annulum, et imponitur ei gremiale a ministris. Tum pollicem suum dexterum intingit in sanctum Chrisma et caput Consecrati coram se genuflexi inungit, formans primo signum crucis per totam coronam, deinde reliquum coronæ liniendo, interim dicens:

Ungátur, et consecrétur caput tuum, cæléсti benedictióne, in órdine Pontificáli.

Et producens manu dextera tertio signum crucis super caput Consecrati, dicit:

In nómine Pa✠tris, et Fí✠lii, et Spíritus ✠ Sancti.
℟. Amen.
℣. Pax tibi.
℟. Et cum spíritu tuo.

Et si plures sint consecrati, hoc in persona cujuslibet singulariter repetit.

Expleta unctione, Pontifex pollicem cum medulla panis paululum abstergit; et finito Hymno prædicto, deposita mitra, surgit et in pristina voce prosequitur dicens:

Hoc, Dómine, copióse in caput ejus ínfluat, hoc in oris subjécta decúrrat; hoc in totíus córporis extréma descéndat, ut tui Spíritus virtus et interióra ejus répleat, et exterióra circúmtegat. Abúndet in eo constántia fídei, púritas dilectiónis, sincéritas pacis. Sint speciósi múnere tuo pedes ejus ad evangelizándum pacem, ad evangelizándum bona tua. Da ei, Dómine, ministérium reconciliatiónis in verbo, et in factis, in virtúte signórum et prodigiórum. Sit sermo ejus, et prædicátio, non in persuasibílibus humánæ sapiéntiæ verbis, sed in ostensióne spíritus et virtútis. Da ei, Dómine, claves regni cælórum, ut utátur, non gloriétur potestáte, quam tríbuis in ædificatiónem, non in destructiónem. Quodcúmque ligáverit super terram, sit ligátum et in cælis, et quodcúmque sólverit super terram, sit solútum et in cælis. Quorum retinúerit peccáta, reténta sint, et quorum remíserit, tu remíttas. Qui maledíxerit ei, sit ille maledíctus, et qui benedíxerit ei, benedictiónibus repleátur. Sit fidélis servus, et prudens, quem constítuas tu, Dómine, super famíliam tuam, ut det illis cibum in témpore opportúno, et exhíbeat omnem hóminem perféctum. Sit sollicitúdine ímpiger, sit spíritu fervens, óderit supérbiam, humilitátem ac veritátem díligat, neque eam umquam déserat, aut láudibus aut timóre superátus. Non ponat lucem ténebras, nec ténebras lucem: non dicat malum bonum, nec bonum malum. Sit sapiéntibus et insipiéntibus débitor; ut fructum de proféctu ómnium consequátur. Tríbuas ei, Dómine, cáthedram episcopálem, ad regéndam Ecclésiam tuam, et plebem sibi commíssam. Sis ei auctóritas, sis ei potéstas, sis ei fírmitas. Multíplica super eum bene✠dictiónem et grátiam tuam: ut ad exorándam semper misericórdiam tuam tuo múnere idóneus et tua grátia possit esse devótus.

Deinde submissa voce dicit legendo, ita quod a circumstantibus audiri possit:

Per Dóminum nostrum Jesum Christum Fílium tuum: Qui tecum vivit et regnat in unitáte Spíritus Sancti Deus, per ómnia sæcula sæculórum.
℟. Amen.

Post hæc Consecrator inchoat, schola prosequente, Antiphonam: Unguéntum in cápite etc. . .

Incepta Antiphona ante Psalmum, imponitur ad collum Consecrati alia ex longioribus mappulis, de octo supradictis. Consecrator sedet; accipit mitram; et Consecrato ante ipsum genuflexo inungit ambas manus simul junctas cum Chrismate in modum crucis, producendo cum pollice suo dextero intincto duas lineas; videlicet a pollice dexteræ manus usque ad indicem sinistræ, et a pollice sinistræ usque ad indicem dexteræ; et mox inungat totaliter palmas Consecrati, dicens:

Ungántur manus istæ de óleo sanctificáto, et Chrísmate sanctificatiónis, sicut unxit Sámuel David Regem et Prophétam, ita ungántur, et consecréntur.

Et producens manu dextera ter signum crucis super manus Consecrati, dicit:

In nómine Dei Pa✠tris, et Fí✠lii, et Spíritus ✠ Sancti, faciéntes . . .

Cetera quæ sequuntur ut in Pontificali Romano.

BIBLIOGRAPHY

Sources

Acta Apostolicae Sedis, Commentarium Officiale, Romae, 1909-1929; Civitate Vaticana, 1929-

Acta et Decreta Concilii Nationalis Armenorum, Romae, 1913.

Acta et Decreta Sacrorum Conciliorum Recentiorum, Collectio Lacensis, 7 vols., Friburgi Brisgoviae, 1870-1892.

Acta Sanctae Sedis, 41 vols., Romae, 1865-1908.

Assisi Papers, The, Proceedings of the First International Congress of Pastoral Liturgy, Collegeville, Minn.: Liturgical Press, 1957.

Bruns, Hermann, *Canones Apostolorum et Conciliorum Saeculorum IV-VII,* 2 vols., Berolini, 1839.

Bullarum Diplomatum et Privilegiorum Sanctorum Pontificum Taurinensis Editio, 24 vols. et Appendix, Augustae Taurinorum, 1857-1872.

Codex iuris Canonici, Pii X Pontificis Maximi iussu degestus, Benedicti Papae XV auctoritate promulgatus, Praefatione, Fontium Annotatione et Indice Analytico-Alphabetico ab Emō Petro Card. Gasparri Auctus, Romae: Typis Polyglottis, 1917; reimpressio, 1949.

Codicis Iuris Canonici Fontes, cura Emī Petro Card. Gasparri editi, 9 vols., Romae: Typis Polyglottis Vaticanis, 1923-1939 (Vols. VII-IX, ed. cura Emī Iustiniani Card. Serédi).

Codificazione Canonica Orientale, Fonti, Serie I, Città del Vaticano: Typis Polyglottis Vaticanis, 1930- ; *Fonti,* Serie II, Città del Vaticano: Typis Polyglottis Vaticanis, 1935- ; *Fontes,* Series III, Città del Vaticano: Typis Polyglottis Vaticanis, 1943- .

Collectanea S. Congregationis de Propaganda Fide, 2 vols., Romae: Typographia Polyglotta S. C. Proganda Fide, 1907.

Concilium Tridentium Diariorum Actorum, Epistularum, Tractatum, Nova Collectio, Edidit Societas Goerresiana, 13 vols., Friburgi Brisgoviae: B. Herder, 1901-

Corpus Iuris Canonici, ed Lipsiensis secunda, post Aemilii Richteri curas instruxit Aemilius Frieberg, 2 vols., Lipsiae, 1879-1881.

Decreta Authentica Congregationis Sacrorum Rituum, 5 vols. et 2 appendices, Romae: Ex Typographia Polyglotta, 1898-1927.

Decretales D. Gregorii Papae IX suae integritati una cum glossis restitutae, 2 vols., Romae, 1582.

Decretum Gratiani, emendatum et observationibus illustratum una cum glossis Gregorii XIII Pont. Max. iussu editum, 2 vols., Romae, 1582.

Enchiridion Symbolorum Definitiorum et Declarationum de Rebus Fidei et Morum, edd. H. Denzinger, C. Banwart, J. Umberg, C. Rahner, 30. ed., Friburgi Brisgoviae: B. Herder, 1955.

Hinchius, Paulus, *Decretales Pseudo-Isidorianae et Capitulae Anglilramni*, Lipsiae, 1863.

Iuris Pontificii de Propaganda Fide Pars Prima, Complectens Decreta, Instructiones, Enclyclicas, Litteras, etc. ab Eadem Congregatione Lata, cura et studio Raphaelis de Martinis, 7 vols. in 8, Romae: Ex Typographia Polyglotta S. C. de Prop. Fide, 1888-1897; *pars Secunda*, 1 vol., Romae, 1909.

Jaffé, Philippus, *Regesta Pontificum Romanorum ab condita Ecclesia ad annum, post Christum natum MCXCVIII*, ed. 2 correctam et auctam auspiciis Gulielmi Wattenback curaverunt F. Kaltenbunner, P. Ewald, S. Loewenfeld, 2 vols., Lipsiae, 1885-1888.

Mansi, J. D., *Sacrorum Conciliorum Nova et Amplissima Collectio*, 53 vols. in 60, Parisiis, 1901-1927.

Ordinarius seu Liber Caeremoniarum ad Usum Sacri et Canonici Ordinis Praemonstratensi, Typis Abbatiae B.V.M. de Tongeloo, 1949.

Pallottini, Salvator, *Collectio omnium conclusionum et resolutionum quae in causis propositis apud Sacrum Congregationem Cardinalium S. Concilii Tridentini Interpretum prodierunt ab eius institutione anno MDLXIV ad annum MDCCCLX, distinctis titulis alphabetico ordine per materias digesta*, 17 vols., Romae, 1868-1893.

Pontificale Romanum Summorum Pontificum jussu editum, a Benedictio XIV et Leone XIII Pontificibus Manimis recognitum et castigatum, Mechliniae, 1895.

Potthast, Augustus, *Regesta Pontificum Romanorum inde ab anno post Christum natum 1198 ad annum 1304*, 2 vols., Berolini, 1874-1875.

Schroeder, H. J., *Canons and Decrees of the Council of Trent*, St. Louis: B. Herder, 1941.

Synodus Alexandrina Coptorum, Romae, 1898.

Synodus Sciarfensis Syrorum, a. 1888, Romae, 1896.

Reference Works

Andrieu, Michel, *Les* ORDINES ROMANI *du Haut Moyen Age*, 3 vols., Louvain: Spicilegium Sacrum Lovaniense, 1931-1951.

———, *Le Pontifical Romain du Moyen Age*, 4 vols., Città del Vaticano: Biblioteca Apostolica Vaticana, 1938-1941.

Bellarminus, St. Robertus, *Omnia Opera*, 6 vols., Neapoli, 1856-1861.

Benedictus XIV, *De Synodo Dioecesana*, 2. ed., 2 vols., Parmae, 1764.

Billot, L., *De Ecclesiae Sacramenti Commentariis in Tertiam Partem S. Thomae*, 2 vols., Vol. I, 7. ed., Romae, 1931; Vol. II, 7. ed., Romae, 1929.

Bligh, John, *Ordination to the Priesthood*, New York: Sheed and Ward, 1956.

Bonaventure, St., *Opera Omnia*, 10 vols., ad Claras Aquas (Quaracchi), 1882-1902.

Cabrol, Fernand, *The Book of the Latin Liturgy,* Translated from the French by the Benedictines of Stanbrook, St. Louis: B. Herder, 1932.

Cappello, Felix, *Tractatus Canonico-Moralis de Sacramentis,* 5 vols., Vol. IV, 3. ed., Taurini-Romae: Marietti, 1951.

Conte a Coronata, Matthaeus, *Institutiones Iuris Canonici, De Sacramentis Tractatus Canonicus,* 3 vols., Vol. II, Editio altera, Torino: Marietti, 1948.

Da Faraese, Giovanni Battista, *Il Sacramento dell' Ordine nel Periodo Precedente la Seccione XXIII di Trento 1515-1562,* Romae: Pontificia Universitas Gregoriana, 1946.

De Castro, Alfonso, *Adversus Omnis Haereses Libri XIV,* Parisiis, 1564.

De Puniet, Pierre, *The Roman Pontifical, A History and Commentary,* Translated by Mildred V. Harcourt, London: Longmans, Green and Co., 1932.

Dix, Gregory, *The Treatise on the Apostolic Tradition of Saint Hippolytus of Rome,* London: Society for Promoting Christian Knowledge, 1920.

Duchesne, Louis, *Christian Worship: Its Origin and Evolution,* 5. ed., Translated by M. L. McClure, London: Society for Promoting Christian Knowledge, 1920.

Eckius, Joannes, *Homiliae sive Sermones adversus Quoscumque Nostri Haereticos,* Coloniae, 1537.

Ellard, Gerald, *Ordination Anointings in the Western Church before 1000 A.D.,* Mediaeval Studies, n. 31: Cambridge, Mass., 1933.

Fagnanus, P., *Commentaria in Quinque Libros Decretalium,* 4 vols., Venetiis, 1709.

Feltoe, C. L., *Sacramentarium Leonianum,* Cambridge: University Press, 1896.

Gasparri, P., *Tractatus Canonicus de Sacra Ordinatione,* 2 vols., Parisiis, 1893.

Guido, Ignazio, *Il Fetha Nagast,* Romae, 1889.

Guido de Baisio, *Rosarium super Decreto,* Venetiis, 1577.

Hallier, F., *De Sacris Electionibus et Ordinationibus ex Antiquo et Novo Ecclesiae Usu,* 2. ed., 3 vols., Romae, 1739.

Hauler, E., *Didascaliae Apostolorum Fragmenta Veronensia,* Lipsiae, 1900.

Hofmann, G., *Documenta Concilii Florentini de Unione Orientalium,* II, *De Unione Armenorum,* Textus et Documenta, Series Theologica, n. 19, Romae: Universitas Gregoriana, 1935.

Hostiensis, Cardinalis (Henricus de Segusio), *In Decretalium Libros Commentaria,* 5 vols. in 3, Venetiis, 1570.

Innocentius IV, *Commentaria super Decretales,* Venetiis, 1570.

Jungmann, Joseph A., *The Mass of the Roman Rite: Its Origins and Development,* translated by Francis A. Brunner, 2 vols., New York: Benziger Brothers, 1950-1955.

Kennedy, Vincent L., *The Saints and the Canon of the Mass,* Studi di Antichità Cristiana, XIV, Città del Vaticano: Pontificio Instituto di Archeologia Cristiana, 1938.

Lennerz, H., *De Sacramento Ordinis,* 2. ed., Romae: Apud Aedea Universitatis Gregorianae, 1953.

Liguori, St. Alphonsus, *Theologia Moralis,* ed. nova cura L. Gaude, 7 libri in 4 vols., Romae, 1905-1912.

Many, Seraphinus, *Praelectiones de Sacra Ordinatione,* Parisiis: Letouzey et Ame, 1905.

Martène, Edmundus, *De Antiquis Ecclesiae Ritibus,* 3 vols., Venetiis, 1783.

Martinucci, Pius-Menghini, I. B. M., *Manuale Sacrarum Caeremoniarum,* in libros octos digestum, 3. ed., 4 vols. Ratisbonae: Pustet, 1911-1915.

McManus, Frederick R., *The Congregation of Sacred Rites,* The Catholic University of America Canon Law Series, n. 352, Washington, D. C.: The Catholic University of America Press, 1954.

Messenger, E. C., *The Reformation, the Mass and the Priesthood,* 2 vols., London–New York–Toronto: Longmans, Green and Co., 1936-1937.

Migne, J. D., *Patrologiae Cursus Completus, Series Latina,* 221 vols., Parisiis, 1844-1864.

Moretti, Aloisius, *Caeremoniale iuxta Ritum Romanum seu De Sacris Functionibus,* 4 vols., Taurini: Marietti, 1936-1939.

Mors, Josephus, *Theologia Fundamentalis,* 2 vols., Bonis Auris, Argentina: Typis "Editorial Gundalupe," 1954.

Muratori, Ludovicus, *Liturgia Romana Vetus,* 2 vols., Venetiis, 1784.

Nabuco, Joachim, *Pontificalis Romani Expositio Juridico-Practica,* 3 vols., Petropoli, Brasilia: Sumptis Editora Vozes Ltda., 1945.

Noldin, Hieronymus–Schmitt, A., *Summa Theologiae Moralis,* 3 vols., Vol. I, 26. ed., 1940, Vols., II-III, 27. ed., 1941, Oeniponte, Lipsiae: F. Rauch.

Oppenheim, Philippus, *Institutiones Systematico-Historicae in Sacram Liturgiam,* Series 1, 6 vols., Taurini-Romae: Marietti, 1937-1941.

Otterbein, Adam, *The Diaconate According to the Apostolic Tradition of Hippolytus and Derived Documents,* The Catholic University of America Studies in Sacred Theology, n. 95, Washington, D. C.: The Catholic University of America Press, 1945.

Panormitanus, Abbas (Nicholaus de Tudeschis), *Commentaria in Quinque Libros Decretalium,* 5 vols. in 7, Venetiis, 1588.

Petrus Lombardus, *Libri IV Sententiarum,* Ad Claras Aquas prope Florentiam, 1916.

Prat, Fernand, *The Theology of Saint Paul,* translated from the 10. French edition by John L. Stoddard, 2 vols., Westminster: The Newman Press, 1952.

Quasten, Johannes, *Patrology,* 3 vols., Westminster, Md.: The Newman Press, 1951-1960.

Raymundus de Peñafort, St., *Summa Aurea,* Romae, 1603.

Regatillo, Edwardus F., *Ius Sacramentarium,* 2. ed., Santander: Sal Terra, 1949.

Reiss, John, *The Time and Place of Sacred Ordination,* The Catholic University of America Canon Law Series, n. 343, Washington, D. C.: The Catholic University of America Press, 1957.

Schuster, Ildefonso, *The Sacramentary, Historical and Liturgical Notes on the Roman Missal,* translated from the Italian by Arthur Levelis-Marke, 5 vols., New York: Benziger, 1924-1930.

Scotus, Joannes Duns, *Opera Omnia,* 26 vols., Parisiis, 1891-1895.

Soto, D., *In IV Sententiarum,* Venetiis, 1538.

Soto, P., *Tractatus de Institutione Sacerdotum,* Dillingae, 1560.

Stehle, Aurelius, *Manual of Episcopal Ceremonies,* 4. ed., Latrobe, Pa.: The Archabbey Press, 1948.

Stevenson, Anthony A., *Anglican Orders,* Westminster, Md.: The Newman Press, 1956.

Tapper, Ruardus, *Opera,* 3 vols., Romae, 1599.

Thomas Aquinas, St., *S. Thomas Opera Omnia,* 25 vols., Parmae: Fiaccodori, 1852-1873.

Tixeront, J., *Holy Orders and Ordination, A Study in the History of Dogma,* Translated from the second French edition by S. A. Raemers, St. Louis–London: B. Herder, 1928.

Van Hove, A., *Commentarium Lovaniense in Codicem Iuris Canonici,* Vol. I, Tom. 1, *Prolegomena,* 2. ed., Mechliniae-Romae: Dessain, 1945.

Van Rossum, G. M., *De Essentia Sacramenti Ordinis,* Editio altera, Romae: Pustet, 1931.

Wernz, F.–Vidal, P., *Ius Canonicum,* 7 vols. in 9, Romae: Apud Aedes Universitatis Gregoriannae, 1923-1938.

Wilson, H., *The Gregorian Sacramentary under Charles the Great,* edited from three Mss. of the ninth century, London, 1915.

Articles

Crosignani, J., "Annotationes ad Constitutionem Apostolicam de Sacris Ordinibus Diaconatus, Presbyteratus et Episcopatus," *Divus Thomas: Commentarium de Philosophia et Theologia,* Series III, XXV (1948), 158-166.

Damen, C., "In Constitutionem *Sacramentum Ordinis* a Pio XII Latam d. 28 ian. 1948: Analysis et Commentarium," *Euntes Docete,* I (1948), 104-111.

De Guibert, J., "Le decret du concile de Florence pour les Armeniens, sa Valeur Dogmatique," *Bulletin de Litterature Ecclesiastique,* X (1919), 81-95, 150-162, 195-216.

Franquesa Adalberto M., "La Constitucion Apostolica acerca de los Obispos Consagrantes," *Revista Española de Derecho Canónico,* II (1947), 211-238.

Hecht, F. X., "De Reparandis Defectibus in Collatione Ordinum Occurrentibus," *Periodica,* XXIII (1934), 73-111.

———, "De Manus Extensione in Ordinatione Diaconali," *Periodica,* XL (1951), 264-270.

Hürth, Franciscus, "Commentarium ad Constitutionem Apostolicam," *Periodica,* XXXVII (1948), 9-40.

Montague, G., "The Apostolic Constitution on Sacred Orders," *Irish Ecclesiastical Record,* 5. series, LXX (1948), 441-446.

Oppenheim, Philippus, "Annotationes ad Constitutionem Apostolicam Episcopalis Consecrationis," *Apollinaris,* XIX (1946), 16-34.

Pujolras, Henricus, "Annotationes," *Commentarium pro Religiosis et Missionariis,* XXIX (1948), 4-11.

Smith, George D., "The Church and Her Sacraments," *The Clergy Review,* XXVIII (1950), 217-231.

Periodicals

Apollinaris, Romae, 1928-

Bulletin de Litterature Ecclesiastique, Toulouse, 1909-

Clergy Review, The, London, 1931-

Commentarium pro Religiosis (later [1935] *Commentarium pro Religiosis et Missionariis*), Romae, 1920-

Divus Thomas: Commentarium de Philosophia et Theologia, Piacenza, Series III, 1924-

Euntes Docete, Romae, 1948-

Irish Ecclesiastical Record, The, Dublin, 1864-

Periodica de Re Canonica et Morali, utilia praesertim Religiosis et Missionariis, Brugis, 1905-1927; *Periodica de Re Morali, Canonica, Liturgica,* Brugis, 1927-1936, Romae, 1936-

Revisita Española de Derecho Canonico, Salamanca, 1946-

ABBREVIATIONS

AAS—*Acta Apostolicae Sedis.*

ASS—*Acta Sanctae Sedis.*

BRT—*Bullarium Romanum, ed. Taurinensis.*

Collectanea—*Collectanea S. Congregationis de Propaganda Fide.*

C. Tr.—*Concilium Tridentinum, Diariorum, Actorum, Epistularum, Tractatuum, Nova Collectio.*

Decr. Auth.—*Decreta Authentica Sacrorum Rituum Congregationis.*

Fontes—*Codicis Iuris Canonici Fontes.*

Fonti—*Codificatione Canonica Orientale, Fonti.*

JE—Jaffé, *Regesta Pontificum Romanorum* (edited by P. Ewald, for the years 590-882).

JK—Jaffé, *op. cit.* (edited by F. Kaltenbrunner, to the year 590).

JL—Jaffé, *op. cit.* (edited by S. Loewenfeld, for the years 882-1189).

Mansi—*Sacrorum Conciliorum Nova et Amplissima Collectio.*

MPL—Migne, *Patrologia, Series Latina.*

Potthast—*Regesta Pontificum Romanorum, etc.*

S.C.S. Off.—Sacra Congregatio Sancti Officii.

S.R.C.—Sacrorum Rituum Congregatio.

ALPHABETICAL INDEX

BIOGRAPHICAL NOTE

Walter Burroughs Clancy was born January 4, 1926, in Helena, Arkansas. He received his elementary and secondary education at Sacred Heart Academy in the same city. In the fall of 1946 he entered St. John's Home Missions Seminary, Little Rock, Arkansas, and four years later was awarded the degree of Bachelor of Arts. He was ordained to the Sacred Priesthood by the Most Reverend Albert L. Fletcher, D.D., Bishop of Little Rock, on May 27, 1954. Thereafter he was appointed to the Faculty of St. John's Home Missions Seminary. In September, 1955, he enrolled in the School of Canon Law of the Catholic University of America, Washington, D. C., from which he received the Baccalaureate Degree in Canon Law in June, 1956, and the degree of the Licentiate in June, 1957.

CANON LAW STUDIES *

392. Adams, Rev. Donald E., A.B., J.C.L., The truth required in the *preces* for rescripts.
393. Bégin, Rev. Raymond F., A.B., S.T.L., J.C.L., Natural law and positive law.
394. Clancy, Rev. Walter B., A.B., J.C.L., The rites and ceremonies of sacred ordination.
395. Cox, Rev. Ronald J., S.T.L., J.C.L., A study of the juridic status of laymen in the writing of the medieval canonists.
396. Demers, Rev. Francis L., O.M.I., A.B., J.C.L., Temporal administration of the religious house in a non-exempt clerical pontifical institute.
397. Dziadosz, Rev. Henry J., M.A., S.T.L., J.C.L., The provisions of the Decree "Spiritus Sancti munera": the law for the extraordinary minister of confirmation.
398. Gerhardt, Rev. Bernard C., A.B., S.T.L., J.C.L., Interpretation of rescripts.
399. Hackett, Rev. John H., A.B., J.C.L., The concept of public order.
400. Murphy, Rev. Richard J., O.M.I., S.T.L., J.C.L., The canonico-juridical status of a communist.
401. O'Connor, Rev. David, M.S.SS.T., J.C.L., Parochial relations and co-operation of the religious and secular clergy.

* For a complete list of the available numbers of this series apply to the Catholic University of America Press, 620 Michigan Avenue, N.E., Washington (17), D. C., for a general catalogue.

www.ingramcontent.com/pod-product-compliance
Lightning Source LLC
LaVergne TN
LVHW050208080826
844660LV00012B/379

* 9 7 8 0 8 1 3 2 2 5 5 4 8 *